The Blueprint

Complete Guide To
Ending The Fur Industry

Peter Young

The bulk of credit for this book goes to those known and unknown, who invested many hours, and often their freedom, to bring the addresses and analysis offered here.

First published in the United States in 2020.

ISBN 978-1732709683

Also published by Warcry:

Flaming Arrows: Collected Writings of Animal Liberation Front Activist Rod Coronado (Rod Coronado)

From Dusk 'til Dawn: An Insider's View of the Growth of the Animal Liberation Movement (Keith Mann)

Underground. The Animal Liberation Front in the 1990s

Liberate: Stories & Lessons On Animal Liberation Above The Law (Peter Young)

Table of Contents

Preface To The Updated Edition

"The Blueprint is…. a terrorist handbook." Utah mink farmer

"A how-to guide for carrying out attacks against mink ranchers." Park Record

At the time *Bite Back Magazine* offered to fund a cross-country trip to visit fur farms in 2009, I was in a quandary over how to contribute to the movement in any high-impact yet non-felonious way. Going to fur farms without any criminal agenda felt deeply incongruous, yet I said yes immediately.

At first, the final output of this trip was unclear. As vaguely outlined, it would involve gathering farm updates for *FinalNail.com*, and an article in *Bite Back* documenting the trip (perhaps focusing on farms that had been past ALF targets, if they were opened or closed, with some possible "convicted fur farm raider returns to the scene of his crimes" sub-plot).

Whatever its ultimate output, the plan was set: Drive to every fur farm in the country, take lots of notes and photos, and make everything public.

While there were certainly more efficient ways to accomplish this (hiring multiple private investigators comes to mind), we couldn't afford those. And other tactics within our budget didn't offer the desired coverage.

Fur farmers have a famously high guard for phone calls (often reporting benign telemarketer calls to the Fur Commission USA as suspected ALF intelligence gathering), so cold calling farms with a social engineering pretext was unlikely to be effective. Likewise, fur farms are so poorly tracked by state and local governments, my formal requests for fur farm lists returned few actual fur farms. Public records requests would be equally unlikely to produce our desired results.

With activism, you often aim for elegance, and settle for "crude but effective." We rented a car and started driving.

In 2009, there was barely a grassroots anti-fur movement to speak of. So, while the audience for an updated fur farm list was small-to-none, if it had a remote chance of inspiring a resurgence, it would be worth the effort.

The demand for this new list was small, it's potential impact unclear, and the effort required to make it massive; yet letting mass numbers of farms continue to exist in comfortable anonymity was not an option.

So, in mid-2009, myself and another person began driving to as many fur farms as possible. Over 2.5 months we visited about 2/3 of the known fur farms in the US. At each stop, we did whatever it took to determine if the farm was open or closed, and took massive amounts of notes.

When it was over, we distilled down the results into one public document: *The Blueprint*. (The full narrative of the "Fur Farm Intelligence Project" was later published in *Bite Back Magazine #15* and even later in my book *Liberate*).

The Blueprint was released in December 2009. Countless hard copies were distributed at animal rights conferences, it was downloaded tens of thousands of times, and it helped introduce to a new generation of activists that the fur industry was comprised of farms and other entities that had physical addresses.

"What to do with this information" was where *The Blueprint* ended and the reader's personal discretion began.

The broader history of fur farm intelligence gathering is traced on page 30, but *The Blueprint*'s place in it was defined in part by the following:

- Dozens of new fur farm addresses made public.
- Operational status of over 200+ farms confirmed.
- Hundreds of new details on fur farms and other industry sites published (specific addresses, notes on layout, species imprisoned, photographs etc).

The Blueprint compiled fur industry addresses, weaknesses, analysis, and specific detail on industry targets that had never been compiled in such detail in one place (the original fur farm list *The Final Nail* deserves original credit for the concept). Much of the details *The Blueprint* contained were either previously scattered, or altogether unknown.

Among the greatest testimonials to the efficacy of efforts like *The Blueprint* came from this paraphrasing of the Fur Commission USA's head of security in *Capital Press*:

"The days of finding security by keeping a low profile in a rural location are over."

After its release, *The Blueprint* had a cascading effect – both direct and speculative. In the former category, it set off a surge of anonymous research, document leaks, and other industry information coming to light at a pace I have not seen in the 15 years I have tracked the industry. Both myself and platforms like *FinalNail.com* received anonymous submissions regularly in the years that followed.

These leaks and new addresses coming to light slowed after 2014. While the Fur Commission continued to direct their attention to threats by activists - distributing branded "No Trespassing" signs to farmers, compiling a (soon leaked) fur farm security guide, telling the media *The Blueprint* was a "terrorists handbook," hiring "security experts" to lock down farms, and generally focusing on "farm security" - they completely missed the economic storm brewing in the distance that would soon bring the US fur farm industry to the brink of collapse (and soon maybe past the brink – the future is unwritten).

The details of this industry meltdown are covered in detail in "The State Of The US Fur Industry" (page 16), but it impacts *The Blueprint* in one huge (and positive) way: A large number of farms contained herein have probably closed after being unable to weather the downturn storm (as of this writing, mink farmers have had to sell pelts at a loss for over four years).

With this recent industry contraction and decrease in farm numbers, a new road trip / investigative campaign is just as needed now as in 2009.

The number of new addresses that have come to light since the original *Blueprint* are massive. This updated *Blueprint* offers many times more new info than the original *Blueprint* (without this editor spending a summer driving to farms).

Here is a rough breakdown of what is new for the updated *Blueprint*:

- 100+ new fur farm addresses.
- 90+ confirmed farm closures.
- 100+ updated details: addresses, owner names, more.
- More detailed analysis of weaknesses.

Whatever leap forward the first *Blueprint* offered, the 10th anniversary update offers in vastly greater numbers.

It seems almost contrived, but work on this 10th anniversary volume began in Sheboygan, Wisconsin; home of the largest mink farm (and a farm where I was personally detained by police two decades prior). Being in Wisconsin on unrelated business intersected with some personal downtime, and I spent a week in Sheboygan's vegetarian cafe to compile every new address and data point from the previous 10 years. There were many.

The majority of entries new to this edition were previously made public in one of a few ways, with *FinalNail.com* being far and away where most new addresses here were first published. In distant second place, *CoaltionAgainstFurFarms.com* (which also hosted two *Blueprint* "supplements"). A full list of credits for the information compiled here (new and old) can be found in "Data Sources" (page 143).

The next generation of anti-fur strategists may find the greatest value in the expanded "Weak Links" chapter, where I go deeper into fur industry vulnerabilities that the original *Blueprint* only touched on.

The power of a weak links together with addresses is that it provides an actionable "blueprint" for deconstruction. The downfall of every animal abuse industry (from foie gras to vivisection) would certainly be served with its own industry-specific *Blueprint*.

If *The Blueprint* accomplishes nothing else, it's this small bit of accountability: There's nowhere to hide, your vulnerabilities are laid bare, and only the reason you still exist is that a small group of dedicated people have yet to apply the knowledge contained here to its maximum impact.

Peter Young
October, 2019
Sheboygan, Wisconsin

How To Use

This document is broken down into three parts, forming a concise blueprint for destroying the fur industry.

The Foundation
Part I details why the fur industry is a weak and strategic target.

The Weak Links
Part II details key vulnerabilities in the fur industry.

The Addresses
Part III is a state-by-state directory of fur farms and infrastructure targets.

Part I

The Foundation

An Endgame Blueprint

How To Destroy The Fur Industry
A Blueprint

This document is a blueprint to destroying one animal abuse industry in the United States.

The fur industry is not the largest animal abuse industry (or the smallest). It is not even the most measurably cruel (despite its savagery, there may still worse fates than being born into a fur farm).

The reason this document exists is that the fur industry is among the weakest.

The Blueprint is the product of thousands of hours of research, of which I am the smallest part. Activists known and unknown have spent years accumulating the data contained here.

They have ferried duffel bags of stolen documents from broken-into buildings, infiltrated fur industry auctions, posed as hitchhikers to infiltrate fur feed delivery routes, and pored over fur industry documents to provide both the addresses and analysis offered here.

Perhaps never has an industry been so thoroughly mapped, and its weaknesses so thoroughly examined, as the fur industry is in the document you're reading.

Operation Bite Back Until Today: Fur Farm Data in the 2000s

The Blueprint brings together all known intelligence about the supply-side of the US fur industry, accumulated over decades.

Prior to this document, the sum of the fur farm addresses we had were dispersed across three sources: The 1st edition of *The Blueprint* (2009), and TheFinalNail.com, and Coalition Against Fur Farms (.com).

Each of these owes credit as their foundation to the original fur farm list, *The Final Nail #1* (1996). For years, the anonymous Final Nail (on its 4th edition as of this writing), and word-of-mouth intel passed among activists, were the only sources of fur industry addresses.

Tracing back the ancestry further brings us to the Operation Bite Back campaign of the early 1990s. In this campaign, several fur research facilities were broken into and were documents removed. While there has never been a proven link between OBB and *The Final Nail #1* that followed, the time-line would hint strongly at a direct lineage.

Concurrent with Operation Bite Back in the early 1990s, we saw the release of sensitive fur industry documents and addresses by a group called Coalition to Abolish Fur Farms. CAFF began to offer a general map of the fur industry via bulletins revealing for the first time addresses of fur farms along with internal industry research documents.

Coalition To Abolish The Fur Trade (CAFT) took this further into the mid-1990s, with a two-pronged outreach effort focused on the public (educating them on fur industry cruelty), and activists (emphasizing targets such as trade shows and industry weak-links like National Fur Foods). In one example, a CAFT volunteer infiltrated International Mink Show in 1994 and authored an anonymous report that is as concise and actionable a guide to industry weak points as one would ever need.

It was both the addresses CAFF and CAFT publicized, and the analysis they offered that serve as the basis for this book (particularly *Part II: Weak Links*).

Fueled by the weakness of the fur industry, additional investigations into hard data (as distinct from its treatment of animals) have taken many forms over many years. Rod Coronado infiltrated the Seattle Fur Exchange (since closed) in the early 1990s, and a decade later activists broke into the Hawkeye Mink Cooperative in Jewel, Iowa by breaking out a window, filling numerous duffel bags, and escaping with thousands of documents.

Without the in-depth analysis of these (known and unknown) activists in the 1990s, we would not know the significance of key components of the industry – from feed to melatonin implants to fur research. They did the hard work. We merely updated the addresses and contextualized it for the current landscape.

Coordinative Outreach and the Actionability of the Address

The basis for the original *Blueprint* in 2009 was simple: While most fur industry investigations focused on the treatment of animals, we took a different angle:

1. Names and addresses.
2. Industry weaknesses.

Of all forms of animal rights outreach, the dissemination of "names and addresses" is at once among the most overlooked, and most potent. To understand the power of the name and address, one must accept a distinction between actionable info, and unactionable.

That which is actionable is information that serves as an immediate call to action. Unactionable data is informative, but offers no clear "next step."

Example: A *Why Vegan?* pamphlet is actionable: the reader can become vegan.

Information becomes less useful the further it moves from being something that can be acted on in an immediate way. A philosophical tome on the socio-economic roots of animal exploitation may be informative, but brings with it no call for action.

For outreach to be useful, it must incite.

An address gives injustice a fixed physical location, and confronts the reader with the obligation that comes with that knowledge. More than knowing of injustice, it is knowing where. The "next step" could be a protest or undercover investigation, but an address brings the burden of action.

Scale-Based Strategy and Blueprints as Bullets

Above the equally horrific meat, dairy, and egg industries, intelligence gathering on the fur industry has a special significance.

By the time of this writing, the industry has shrunk to fewer than 350 supply-end sites. Fewer than 350 physical locations form the physical architecture of the entire fur industry. We have arrived at the stage the entire industry can be easily mapped into one concise blueprint.

While a blueprint assists construction, it brings equal utility to deconstruction.

The Architecture of Avarice

The current farm and support structure of the U.S. fur industry (numbers approximate):

Processors / wholesalers / etc: numbers unknown.
Mink farms: 268 (at the last time the USDA gathered statistics)
Feed suppliers: +/- 20
Equipment suppliers (cages, etc): 10
Research farms: +/-3
Processing plants: 1

That is it. And the end of the industry does not require the erasure of every target, only its support structure.

Choke Points And The Scale /Absorption Quotient

The further one moves upstream to industry choke-points, the higher-impact the target. Fewer than 300 mink farms are supported by only a very small and vulnerable support-base of research farms and feed suppliers.

A comprehensive industry map, with details of its supply and support structure, allows an immeasurably greater ability to identify weaknesses that will bring its collapse.

Were you, tonight, to pore over a list of thousands of chicken farms, chicken slaughterhouses, chicken feed producers, chicken research labs, and chicken distributors, it would be impossible to identify anything you could do that moment to remove a pillar from the industry and bring it measurably closer to collapse.

In the fur industry, such pillars number in the low-dozens.

The fur industry is on the losing end of the scale / absorption quotient, whereby the effect of any one action is inversely proportional to an industry's mass. In a large industry, no one target takes on major significance in the supply network – there is always another target that fulfils the same role, and quickly absorbs any business from a decommissioned building or bankrupt processor.

The fur industry is the opposite. Farms generally have only one choice for specialized feed. Industry research sites number at approximately five. Farms rely on breeding stock with genetic lines that are irreplaceable. From every angle, the industry is weak.

The Blueprint is a concise guide to its collapse.

A-K Moyle Ranch; Wendell, Idaho

Part II

Weak Links

The Six Vulnerabilities

The State Of The US Fur Industry

As this goes to press, the US mink industry is in a meltdown.

In 2009, when the first edition of *The Blueprint* was published, the "ranch mink" industry was approaching an all time high for pelt prices.

As of this writing, mink skins are selling for just around $25 – a record low.

After 2013, prices went into a freefall, dropping almost 50% in a single year. When you consider the average cost to raise a mink until pelting season is $35 to $42, the value of a mink dropping to $25 has sent the entire industry is in an insolvent panic. Today, farmers losing money each year the prices remain below their costs.

To quote a recent NAFA letter to the industry, the entire fur industry is at "unprofitable levels across all facets of the trade."

Perhaps the only farmers who have been able to weather the storm are either those who have a sizeable war chest allowing them to operate at a loss for years in a row, those with financial backers to float them through the downturn, or those who have figured out to get costs per mink below $25 (if that is even possible).

In the last year tracked by the USDA, the value of the total mink "crop" from 2017 to 2018 dropped 33%.

A few symptoms of the North American fur industry's collapse:

1. Pelt prices have been below break-even point since 2015.
2. American Legend shuts down. The only fur auction house of significance in the United States shut down in 2018 and was acquired by North American Fur Auctions.
3. Then North American Fur Auctions itself became insolvent. Their bank severed ties, and sent NAFA into the Canadian equivalent of bankruptcy protection.
4. US fur exports from 2013 to 2018 are down 72%.

5. Unconfirmed fur industry chatter has it that "at least half if not more" of mink farms in Canada and "to a lesser extent" in the US have shut down.

What happens when fur farms are forced to pelts at a loss?

When a farm can't survive, it "pelts out," i.e. kills every animal and closes down. However that may not be the end of the story for these farms.

If the industry rebounds in the future, closed farms are likely to be the first to reenter the business. They'll be forced to purchase new breeding stock at a steep cost, but pelting out until an industry upturn may in fact be the strategy for many farms.

For this reason, *The Blueprint* includes a "closed farm list" of all farms known to have closed in the decade prior to publication. These farms should not written out of history, as they may reemerge to imprison animals once again.

What is causing this fur industry meltdown?

The biggest factor is "overproduction," in both the US and internationally.

After the price peak of $100 per pelt in 2013, many countries ramped up their breeding. Many newer farms opened in the US and abroad, and existing US farms increased production by almost 1 million animals from 2010 to 2015. ,China alone doubled their production to nearly 40 million pelts.

This overproduction is the chief driver of the current turmoil.

Other factors include lower demand in China due to warmer winters and reduced "luxury" spending, and economic turbulence decreasing demand in Russia.

There is one thing consistent among all communications in the fur industry that happen when they don't think outsiders are watching: An undertone of panic.

The future is unwritten, but even leaders in the industry have abandoned optimism on the future of the US fur industry.

The time is now

Across every pillar in the fur industry's support structure, now more than ever, the slightest nudge could bring them to collapse.

As of this writing, the US fur farming industry is at its weakest point. The weak links have never been weaker.

Any impact on the profits of a farm, a feed supplier, or any company that depends on the fur industry is likely to put it out of business.

That means that now more than ever is the time to act.

Mink Average Price Per Pelt – United States

Dollars

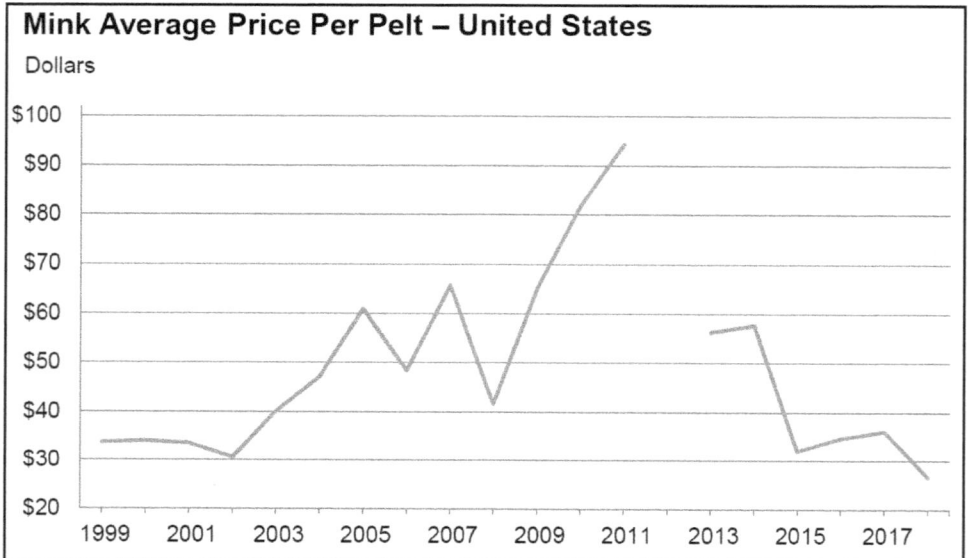

Weak Link #1
Feed Suppliers

Feed cost is the largest cost incurred by fur farms, representing 50-60 percent of the total cost of producing a pelt.

Small increases in feed costs, or the loss in feed supply, can (and have) forced farms out of business.

In a letter to the to the FDA from Dale Lawson of Northwest Farm Food, he states that without inexpensive and specialized feed ensuring top pelt quality, the U.S. fur industry would collapse.

"The additional costs associated with [FDA proposal leading to increase in feed costs] would, in my opinion, totally eliminate the mink industry in the United States."

A farmer speaking this candidly about the critical role of feed is not uncommon. I have viewed other industry literature laying bare this reality of fur farming in the US: With other countries now able to produce fur more cheaply than the US, the only way US farmers can compete and the only edge they have in the global market is superior pelt quality. And along with breeding stock, the most crucial factor in pelt quality is specialized feed.

In Utah, when the Fur Breeder's Agricultural Co-op stopped delivering to their town, several farms were forced to close.

Studying patterns of the most fur farm closures, among the states with either no remaining farms or a rapid decline in farms, one pattern is clear: Where feed must be imported long distances (thus increasing costs), farms tend to close.

With only a handful of significant feed supplier targets, there may be no weaker link in the fur industry.

The current breakdown of known U.S. feed suppliers

Confirmed large suppliers
Medford Fur Foods (WI)
United Feeds (WI)

National Feeds (WI)
Northwest Farm Food-Burlington (WA)
Northwest Farm Food-Astoria (OR)
Fur Breeder's Agricultural Co-op: Logan (UT)
Fur Breeder's Agricultural Co-op: Sandy (UT)
Heger Company (MN)

Smaller suppliers or suppliers whose size or operational status is unknown

Western Pennsylvania Fur Farmers Cooperative Association (PA)
Shoreline Feeds (UT)
Central Mink Foods (WI)
Wisco Feed (WI)
Rancher's Choice (fox feed) (NE)
Hawkeye Mink Cooperative (one time large supplier, current status unknown) (IA)
Alpine Clean Food (ID)
Midwest Ingredients (IL)
North Central Companies (MN)
Mazuri / Purina Mills (MO)
BHJ USA (NE)
Heartland Blends (NE)
LaBudde Group, Inc. (WI)

Fur Breeder's Agricultural Co-op, Sandy UT

Weak Link #2
Processing Plants

This entry almost didn't make it into *The Blueprint*: As this goes to print, the only large-scale processor in the US – North American Fur Auctions – has sought bankruptcy protection in Canada and was on the brink of collapse before its Wisconsin facility was taken over by Saga Furs of Finland.

The North American Fur Auctions / Saga facility in Stoughton, Wisconsin represents the biggest choke point in the US fur industry — a single building through which passes the skins of over a million animals annually.

NAFA become even more significant in 2018 when it acquired American Legend, the only other large scale processor.

Each year, the majority of "ranch" skins pass through their facility southeast of Madison. Both farmers and trappers ship their skins to NAFA. Once there, the pelts are processed and graded, and then (most) are shipped to Canada to be auctioned.

The significance of this facility cannot be overstated. A majority of the animals killed on US fur farms pass through one building in a narrow several-month period after pelting season (generally December).

Were it's Stoughton processing facility to cease to exist, it's not clear how US fur farmers would process their mink and fox skins; or how the industry itself will survive.

What we know about the NAFA facility

NAFA has two buildings across the street from each other in Stoughton, Wisconsin.

North American Fur Auctions
205 Industrial Park Drive
Stoughton, WI 53589
Phone: (608) 205-9200
Fax: (608) 205-9210
(608) 207 3884 (cell)
(608) 205 9210 (fax)

While the recent NAFA takeover by Saga Furs and the passage of time are likely to result in staff reduction and turnover, here is a partial list of last known employees & positions:

Doug Lawson: President and CEO
Denis Schmitt: VP Ranch (fur farm) Relations)
Greg Schroeder: US Trapper Relations Manager
Mike Balaam: Manager
Craig Oler: Maintenance / Supervisor
Laura Chicaizza: Assistant Manager
Brett Johnson: Maintenance Manager
Virgil Schroeder: Wild Fur Coordinator
Jim Posch: Mink Technical Manager
Dave Mengar: Shipping
Carmen Torres: Receiving
Amanda Bujosa: Ticketing
Mark Kubitz: Mink
Joe Poquette: Mink
Tom Gibson: Mink
Brian MacMillan: Wild Fur

Processing & pelt grading facility, Stoughton, WI

Weak Link #3
Fur Industry Research

The industry's research apparatus is part of its central support structure.

Each year, the Research Committee of the Fur Commission USA (aka "Mink Farmer's Research Foundation") funds research projects to increase fur farmer profits and keep the industry afloat.

Most fur industry research targets have been raided, burned down, or otherwise sabotaged by the Animal Liberation Front. The raids have succeeded in disrupting research, saving animals, and confiscating data, but only one — Oregon State University — has been shut down directly by the efforts of activists.

Most of the major research farms dedicated to mink research have been confirmed closed for other reasons, or are believed to have closed. Those include:

- National Feeds: Formerly operated a "research ranch" in Oshkosh, WI. If the farm was relocated, its current location is unknown.
- Utah State University: One-time hub of Aleutian disease research under LeGrand Ellis, Ellis died in 2008 and there has been no recent evidence mink research at USU continues.
- Numerous other research farms at the University of Wisconsin, Oregon State University, and New York University have all been reported as closed.

A closer look at the remaining fur industry research targets:

Confirmed In Operation

Idaho State University

Dr. Jack Rose has been a large recipient of research grants from the Fur Commission USA "to support his studies on delayed implantation in mink." His focus is on research related to mink reproduction.

It is reported the Jack Rose obtains his mink from one of the Moyle mink farms.

While it would seem unlikely research to benefit the fur farming industry would be done in an indoor laboratory setting, all attempts at finding an off-campus ag-research farm were unfruitful, and surveys of the outlying areas of campus failed to located mink sheds – if they exist.

One report places animal research Jack Rose's department in the basement of the Biology building, and it is possible his mink research is performed there.

The fur industry deems Dr. Rose's research to be worthy of a significant percentage of its budget, and should be assumed to be vital to the continued survival of the fur industry.

Near the top of the "must locate" list.

Michigan State University Fur Animal Research Station

Off Jolly Road in Lansing, Michigan State University operates an experimental fur farm "where research on nutrition, physiology, toxicology and management of fur bearing animals is conducted." The latest information states, "The present Experimental Fur Farm can accommodate over 1,000 research animals."

Former head researcher Richard Aulerich retired in 2002, yet the farm is very much still in operation. The facility, and head researcher Dr. Steve Bursian, continue to receive grants from the Fur Commission USA.

Research Farms That May Be Closed (Investigation Needed)

Washington State University

The most uncertain of possible closures, this former hub of mink research has made claims to the media it no longer does mink research on campus.

Quote: "WSU has not conducted any animal-based research for the fur industry in many years"

It appears the university is trying to get off on a technicality in qualifying their statement as referring only to "animal based research." Fur Commission USA documents confirm a 2013 research grant to WSU's John Gorham (now retired).

While head mink researcher John Gorham is gone, his protégé David J. Prieur continues to work at WSU. Prieur has also received funding from the Mink Farmer's Research Foundation.

Curiously, WSU has another fur industry connection: The Fur Commission USA's "directory of public affairs," Jason Roesler, is also a professor at WSU.

For more information on research at Washington State University, see an anonymously submitted report in the address directly.

Claims from the university they are out of the mink research business (made in the context of media coverage on being targeted by activists) should be taken as extremely suspect, and it warrants further investigation whether mink research at WSU continues.

Utah Fur Breeder's Cooperative

Behind the largest fur feed cooperative in the country sits an experimental farm. Partially visible from 700 West, these sheds are the site of feed research to benefit the Utah fur industry at the direction of Austin E. Larsen. The Utah FBAC has been the recipient of many Mink Farmer Research Foundation grants in the past.

There is some uncertainty as to the operational status of this research farm. One unconfirmed report from within the fur industry stated that animals are no longer held at this location, and investigation is needed.

National Feeds

Yet another research farm the existence of which is very much in question.

National Feeds was known for many years (and is still likely to be) the largest fur farm feed supplier in the US. At one time, it operated a research farm in Oshkosh, Wisconsin that held 4,000 mink. It was the industry's largest and most advanced fur research facility.

It is confirmed the farm is no longer at its former location. What is not confirmed with 100% certainty is that the farm no longer exists at all. Complicating this confirmation further, National Feeds is a private company that is not likely to be the recipient of public grants, and as such is going to leave fewer clues of its existence.

There is no question fur farm feed is no longer as profitable as it once was, but whether National Feed has abandoned mink research altogether is not certain.

More vital research

More grants have also been given to various veterinarians, companies, and local fur farming organizations; in addition to the existence of a small amount of private research. These include:

- American Fur Merchants Association (New York, NY)
- Olympic Fur Breeders (Granite Falls, WA)
- Kettle Moraine Mink Breeders (Plymouth, WI)
- Dr. John Easley (Plymouth, WI). Easley is a leading expert in mink disease.
- Dr. Hugh Hildebrandt, Medford Veterinary Clinic (Medford, WI) Hildebrandt is the editor of *Fur Farm Research Letter* (quarterly publication of the Fur Commission USA).
- Dr. Bernhard Benkel, Canadian Mink Breeders Association
- Dr. Robert L. Stephon, Scintilla Development Company (Provides Aleutian Disease Virus testing for mink farmers, and is said to do its research at the Michigan State University Fur Animal Research Station) (Bath, PA)
- United Vaccines (Verona, WI). Experiments on live mink at an unknown location, believed to be in Blue Mound, WI.

Weak Link #4
Aleutian Disease

In a Fur Farm Letter poll, mink farmers named Aleutian disease as their second greatest fear, after attacks by animal rights activists.

Aleutian disease has wiped out countless farms. It is highly transmittable, and once a farm is infected, it spreads rapidly through the mink population.

As one Utah farmer stated, "It's like AIDS for minks." The analogy isn't the best, because Aleutian disease is highly transmissible, not requiring without animal-to-animal contact.

Because of the ease of transmission, farms infected with Aleutian disease face many challenges.

One, they become instant pariahs in the fur farming world. Feed suppliers won't even deliver to farms with mink that have tested positive for Aleutian disease out of fear the delivery trucks will transmit to other farms via truck tires or worker gloves. Any farm that tests positive finds it is shut off from the rest of the fur industry.

Two, they must "pelt out" and start over. Any farm with a trace of Aleutian disease in it heard will quickly find the rest of the heard infected.

Three, they must disinfect the entire property. This is a long an expensive process. All nesting boxes must be destroyed and repurchased, cages must be disinfected, and any object on the farm that may be contaminated must be disposed of and repurchased.

I observed a large farm in Wild Rose, WI I believed had been recently wiped out by Aleutian disease, and the scene was indistinguishable from a farm under construction: cranes were present, all sheds gutted, and towers of new, shrink-wrapped nesting boxes dotted the property.

Many (if not most) farms that become infected never recover and are forced to shut down.

How to target the weak link

Amplify news of farms infected with Aleutian disease. While this information is hard to obtain, any news that a farm is infected should be publicized. Farms may try to conceal infections from the rest of the industry from fear of losing business.

Target Aleutian disease research. Today, most Aleutian disease research is done in Canada. And most of the leading Aleutian disease researchers in the US have retired (John Gorham @ Washington State University, LeGrande Ellis @ Utah State University).

Who is currently active in US Aleutian disease research?

1. Dr. Hugh Hildebrandt, Medford Veterinary Clinic (Medford, Wisconsin): Developed a test for AD.
2. Dr. Robert L. Stephon, Scintilla Development Company (Bath, PA): Also doing research on tests for AD. Research is reportedly done at the MSU experimental fur farm.
3. Branson W. Ritchie, College of Veterinary Medicine, University of Georgia, (Athens, GA): Heading the Mink Genome Project. This project aims to alleviate the industry of Aleutian disease via cell mediated research to isolate mink genes that are resistant to AD.
4. John Easley, Dairy Doctors Veterinary Services (Plymouth WI): Leading expert in mink disease.

Weak Link #5
Melatonin Implants

To the farms that use them, melatonin implants provide them a massive cost-saving advantage.

Melatonin implants causes the fur of mink to develop quicker, allowing farmers to kill the animals in October instead of December.

A mink consumes an average of 64 pounds of feed in its lifespan, and melatonin implants reduce that to 52 pounds. This is a 19% reduction in feed costs, with feed being the single biggest expense in raising mink.

There is only one known melatonin implant supplier.

Neo-Dynamics is registered in Colorado, but has a related address in Middleton, WI.

> Neo-Dynamics
> 4738 Bergamot Way, Suite 200
> Middleton, WI 53562
> Phone: (800) 206-7227
> Fax: (608) 831-4669
> Contact: Tim J. Cairns

According to the Colorado Secretary of State, the company's "Principal Street Address" is:

> 625 N Taft Hill Rd
> Fort Collins, CO 80521

Neo-Dynamics is also associated with these Fort Collins-area addresses:

> 170 Chopp Court
> Bellevue, CO 80512

> 1654 Northbrook Dr
> Fort Collins, CO 80526

It is possible the drug is manufactured in Colorado, but marketed out of Wisconsin.

This is the same company as (or a new incarnation of) Wildlife Pharmaceuticals, a manufacturer of melatonin implants since the mid-1990s.

Cairns is also a current or former fox farmer.

Weak Link #6
Vaccines

When mink farmers don't have access to vaccines, they panic. Gauging from fur industry literature, vaccines are essential to the survival of the US fur industry.

Vaccines provide protection against such diseases as distemper, virus enteritis, botulism and bacterial pneumonia and are usually administered before the mink are 10 weeks old.

For years, the US fur industry had two main suppliers: Merck, and United Vaccines.

After Merck suffered a vaccine production shortage in 2012, representatives from the US mink industry were so concerned; they traveled to the Merck research facility outside Omaha to meet with the company to prevent future shortages.

The following year, the company stopped producing mink vaccines, leaving the US mink industry in the dangerous position of having just one vaccine supplier: United Vaccines.

Today, United Vaccines is key to the survival of the US fur industry.

It is possible there may be no weaker link: Unlike feed suppliers or researchers, there is no replacement for United Vaccines. Without it, there are no mink vaccines, forcing kit mortality up and profits down.

Mink farmers simply have nowhere left to go.

Having what appears to be a monopoly on mink vaccines (information on international suppliers is scarce and international vaccine sources are not known), business is brisk for United Vaccines: In 2018, they relocated to a larger facility in Verona, WI; outside Madison.

What is known about United Vaccines

United Vaccines may have three locations. While at their previous facility in

Fitchburg, WI; the USDA reported inspections at two other sites: One in Verona, WI (where they have since relocated), and another in Blue Mounds, WI (just west of Verona).

It is unclear where the mink research takes place, however there is evidence it is not performed at their main facility (where they claim to only do research on mice and "other rodents.") One USDA inspection report references mink research in either Blue Mounds or Verona (since their current Verona facility was constructed after the report, the location referenced was not their current facility).

Mink Veterinary Consulting and Research Service (MVCRS)

As further evidence of the importance of vaccines, US mink farmers have established a 501c3 non-profit called "Mink Veterinary Consulting and Research Service" to procure vaccines at a discount. Headed by mink disease expert John Easley, the stated purpose of the organization is "assisting with the coordination of critical vaccine supply."

They pool fur farmer capital ($7 million in 2013) to make an annual bulk purchase from United Vaccines and distribute to fur farmers.

It's board members are John Easley, Gerald Trimberger, Brad Joyner, Scott Harris, and Thomas Mclellan.

Anything that can be done to stop United Vaccines would be a major – perhaps unrecoverable – blow to the US mink industry.

Part III

The Addresses

Fur Farms & Their Support Structure

Key:

FF-M: Mink fur farm
FF-F: Fox fur farm
FF-MISC: Other species
FFO: Fur farming organization
FR: Fur industry research
FFES: Fur farm equipment supplier
FFFS: Fur farm feed supplier

Fur Industry Research: A Personal History

I remember where I was when I learned of the power of an address.

In 1996, I boarded a Greyhound from Seattle to Minneapolis, perceived as a hub of mid-90s animal rights activism. (While I've since learned the movements and campaigns that seem large from a distance are often less-impressive up close, Minneapolis at the time did have a vibrant group.)

Local organizer Freeman Wicklund took me to a meeting for the group Student Organization for Animal Rights. As the meeting began, a woman passed out a copy of *The Final Nail #1*.

The meeting became background noise as I read every page of the "Guide to Destroying the Fur Industry." For the first time, it was all in one place: The how-to of hitting industry weak points, and the where-to of fur farm addresses. While *The Blueprint* does not delve into the extra-legal tactics of *The Final Nail, The Blueprint* does owe its general framework (and much of its content) to that photocopied manual handed to me in 1996.

It's not easy to capture work as an activist in the pre-internet age. The scarcity of information can't be adequately conveyed. To have even a single address of an animal abuser was a rare treasure of both possibility and responsibility.

To have over 200 addresses was a point of no return.

The power of the "name and address"

Within a few months of returning home, I was visiting the Seattle-area addresses published in *The Final Nail*. (Often unsuccessfully – my first visit to a fur farm in Granite Falls ended in a foot chase.)

There was a burden that came with knowing where injustice was occurring, and several trusted friends and I accepted that burden.

Shortly after this in-person reconnaissance began, I attended a Thanksgiving vegan potluck. A group of activists had just moved from Salt Lake City (one of them charged with burning down a McDonalds), and brought with them the brand new *Final Nail Supplement* – containing new information on fur farm security, and more importantly, dozens of new addresses.

With the number of new addresses in *The Final Nail Supplement*, I was made aware how many more farms awaited discovery. I made it my mission to find them.

One of my early attempts was a group effort to find street addresses for the mink farms in Astoria Oregon. One defect in *The Final Nail* address list was that, for many farms, it only listed a "rural route" address. The cruellest tease of the fur farm surveillant, a "rural route" was used by postal workers only, and almost impossible to link to a street address. A "rural route" only told you the farm existed – it didn't tell you where.

Several friends and I spent all night driving up and down seemingly every road in Astoria. By night's end, the location of Astoria's multiple mink farms remained elusive.

The Final Nail remained the last and only stop for fur farm addresses – for awhile.

On the road

A year later, a friend and I made a decision. Limited by our still-small skillset and equally undeveloped confidence, we decided (unwisely & prematurely) that we had exhausted our options to release animals from Seattle-area mink farms. Our assessment at the time was that the easy targets were on alert after being raided by activists (sometimes multiple times), others provided no viable parking options (making getting close a challenge), and still others had electronic security we had tried to circumvent but still triggered (leading to more than one close call).

To address these challenges, we plotted a cross-country campaign to the largest mink farming state in the US: Wisconsin.

We bought a car and drove east.

With only the spotty information in *The Final Nail* as our guide, and no internet to rely on, we had to get creative.

In every area with a concentration of fur farms, we spent hours in the library, buried in phone directories, looking up farmer's last names for street addresses. From there, we visited false lead after false lead, yielding the occasional undiscovered farm. Sometimes it was as simple as taking an unplanned turn down any road with the word "mink" or "fur" in its name (e.g. "Fur Farm Road").

Our research was a little *too* successful: After our limited options in the Northwest, we were unprepared for the abundance of options the Midwest offered. We released animals at six farms in two weeks, were pulled over near the largest mink farm in the country with a car of burglary tools and *The Final Nail*, were charged with Animal Enterprise Terrorism, and I became a fugitive for eight years. But that's a different story.

Our notes from that trip were confiscated by the FBI, and other than what was etched into my memory, I feared they would be lost forever.

Research from the underground

Now a fugitive, I continued to do my part in discovering additional addresses as my research continued – from the safe side of fur farm property lines. But without the internet, or knowing the anonymous authors of *The Final Nail*, I had no platform to distribute this information.

18 months into my fugitive life, a trusted friend and I attended the 1999 reunion show of a band called Vegan Reich. There, this friend arranged a meeting with another activist who was said to be working with the anonymous *Final Nail* authors on an updated edition. Knowing of my legal predicament and that I likely had new info to contribute, we spent hours talking – him sharing what new fur farm information him and his group had compiled, and me sharing what I knew.

(Another edition of *The Final Nail* wouldn't come out for another nine years. But when it did, the info I had shared was included – nearly a decade later.)

There was logic behind this obsessiveness of many activist's research into the fur industry: Unlike most industrialized animal agriculture, the fur farm industry was small enough that it could be completely mapped, its weak links isolated, and those weak links targeted.

While mapping the meat industry might feel so daunting as to be futile, mapping the fur industry was small enough to make it doable, and consequently, to make defeating it winnable.

Digital recon

As the internet advanced, its utility in fur farm research did not increase at the same pace. Fur farming is such a small, off-the-grid industry, most farms exist without any digital trace. Yet the internet did evolve to offer some key benefit to fur farm intelligence gathering.

When the first free online business-to-business directories went live, my first search was for farms in a town that I had a personal vendetta with: Astoria, Oregon. After those many futile hours driving its back roads looking for mink farms, this business directory turned up four unknown Astoria farm addresses in mere seconds.

(It seems that either online directories got worse, fur farmers got smarter, or the list of known fur farms got better, because unknown fur farm addresses in today's online directories are scarce, and don't come close to the internet's early days).

Perhaps the greatest benefit to fur farm research the internet has offered is satellite imagery. In the early-2000s, I learned of the first (?) website allowing you to view zoomed-in aerial images of any town or property (this was pre-Google maps — if I recall, this was a NASA-operated site). These aerial images were immensely valuable to the discovery of new mink farms for a specific reason: While other species of farmed animals were confined in structures of interchangeable size and shape, mink farm sheds were almost invariably distinct: much smaller, much narrower, never featuring attached feed silos (obligatory among most other types of farms), and averaging many more sheds per property than any other. Once you knew what a mink farm looked like from above, they were impossible to miss.

With the introduction of satellite images, you could pick a town, and aerially scan the town in a few minutes. This aided in both the discovery of new farms, and the ability to remotely verify existing addresses without the burden of an in-person visit.

Satellite images were not flawless. While mink farms have a distinct layout, I learned the hard way they also share a layout with other structures. In one instance, what satellite images indicated was a small mink farm in Minnesota revealed itself at 1am to be a storage facility for boats. In another, the "mink farm" turned out to be another kind of business altogether: a puppy mill. And when we were certain we had discovered the largest undiscovered mink farm in the country near Salem, Oregon; we showed up to find a massive hydroponic flower-growing operation.

Throughout my fugitive years, motivated by my aboveground contacts who could disseminate new information to the broader movement (in ways that I couldn't while in hiding); I continued my offline research as well.

In one instance, a friend and I drove to a farm in Kimball, Minnesota six months after activists had released 4,000 mink from its cages. We found the farm had totally closed. Probing deeper, we found its offices gutted except for a desk containing some paperwork. In addition to copies of *Fur Rancher Magazine* (a rich source of info in the 1990s) we found various documents with several undiscovered fur farm addresses.

(One of these documents indicated the farm had an undiscovered second location, described only as "the Pearl Lake ranch." We tried zealously to find this farm, unsuccessfully. After a decade of this unresolved mystery, the volunteers at FinalNail.com recently located it.)

Every time I learned of a new fur farm address, I would distribute it to trusted contacts who would distribute it further. And with some regularity, I would observe from a distance that addresses I had disseminated would—in one form or another—be put to good use.

Resurrection

Many years passed, and a 3rd edition of *The Final Nail* had yet to surface. By the time I was arrested and sent to prison in 2005, it had been almost 10 years since the last *Final Nail*. I feared that the addresses myself and others had unearthed and dispersed would never be formally organized and released.

Finally, in 2008, the 3rd edition of *The Final Nail* appeared anonymously online. With dozens of new addresses, it was a long awaited relief to see an update. *The Final Nail #3* enjoyed only limited circulation, and without a vibrant anti-fur movement to amplify it, it did not enjoy the traction of its predecessors. What it did do was finally make public many of the addresses that had been floating among activists via word of mouth and typed-up lists for many years.

(Much credit goes to FinalNail.com [which has no relationship to the print-version of *The Final Nail*] for also publicizing a huge amount of new information even before *The Final Nail #3*.)

The Fur Farm Intelligence Project

While new and improved, there was a significant gap in the fur farm list: How many of these farms were still open? With close to 500 farms in the mid-90s, by 2008 the USDA reported that number had dropped by around 40%. There were many newly discovered farms, but almost no new intel on their operational status. Outside of A.L.F. raids, the "open" or "closed" status of each farm were rarely verified.

Now out of prison, I honed in on this gap in the existing fur farm list: An unmet need to discover which farms had closed, and which were still open.

In 2009, I organized a solution to close these (and other) gaps in fur farm intelligence: a two-month road trip to every fur farm in the western U.S.

The goal: compile the largest collection of raw fur industry data to date. Which farms were open, and which were closed, and come as close as possible to mapping the entire fur industry.

We called it the Fur Farm Intelligence Project. Our mission statement:

"To compile the largest-ever collection of hard data on fur farms and fur industry infrastructure. To map the entire industry, with a primary focus on names, addresses, and other actionable data."

I drafted a budget. *Bite Back Magazine* wrote a check. And the Fur Farm Intelligence Project came to life.

I recruited Daisy as a road trip partner. We spent two months scanning satellite images in fur farming regions. We cross-referenced every fur farm address collection (primarily *The Final Nail #3* and FinalNail.com). We assembled a binder of maps. We compiled lists of unverified addresses mined from media reports, fur industry literature, and the word-of-mouth stream. Then we left on the Fur Farm Intelligence Project (FFIP), a mission to document and verify 75%+ of the fur farms in the U.S.

The information we gathered on this trip, combined with multiple other sources, became the first edition of *The Blueprint*.

We were successful in our mission. The first *Blueprint* was the largest leap forward in fur farm intelligence since *The Final Nail #1*.

From 2009 until today

The Blueprint inspired a small surge of anonymous research, document leaks, and other industry information coming to light at a pace I have not seen in the 15 years I have tracked the industry.

From volunteers at FinalNail.com publishing the bulk of new information in the form of hundreds of new addresses and updates, to large numbers of anonymous submissions — after the publication of *The Blueprint,* new information came in at such a fast pace, tracking it all became a challenge.

So I created a website — CoalitionAgainstFurFarms.com (a nod to Coalition To Abolish Fur Farms, a group that publicized fur industry data in the early 90s) — and updated it with all significant new information as it came in.

I published two supplements to *The Blueprint* over the next several years, with even more new fur farm addresses, closures, and more.

The updated *Blueprint* you're reading is the culmination of all data collected by the animal rights movement since the 1990s – every known address, every key player, and every weakness.

The burden of knowledge

With this document, you are able to shortcut past all the labor expended to compile it — all the 2am farm trespassing, dumpster diving for documents, felony burglaries, hundreds of hours of satellite image scanning, analysis of industry research documents, and industry conference infiltration — and skip to the most important part...

What to do with it.

Fur Farm Address List

Georgia

Branson W. Ritchie (FR)
Department of Small Animal Medicine
College of Veterinary Medicine
University of Georgia
Athens, GA
Notes: Fur industry researcher. From a Fur Farm Intelligence Unit statement: "Richie has volunteered his research skills to the mink industry as part of the proposed Mink Genome Project. This project aims to alleviate the industry of one of its biggest threats: aleutian disease. He has offered cell mediated research to isolate mink genes that are resistant to AD. This research will be done in partnership with Dr. John Easley of Plymouth, Wisconsin, who is also a leading expert in mink disease. Ritchie is awaiting funding from the Fur Commission USA's research committee before the Mink Genome Project is launched." Aleutian disease is a major threat to fur farms.

Idaho

Total mink imprisoned (2019 USDA statistics): 372,000

Geary Fur Farm (FF-M)
425 S 400 W
Burley, ID 83318
Phone: (208) 678-3327
Contact: Jed & Treena Geary
Notes: Located at southeast intersection of 400 S and S 400 W.

Warner & Sons (FF-M)
125 S 350 E
Burley, ID 83318
Phone: (208) 678-8642
Contact: Gary Warner
Notes: Located southeast corner of S 350 E and E. Highway 81. Farm may be closed (investigation needed).

Moyle Mink Ranch (FF-M)
571 E. Highway 81
Burley, ID 83318
Contact: Don Moyle, Cindy Moyle, Mark Moyle
Phone: (208) 654-2033
Notes: Located off Highway 81, south on S 600 E to end of road. Cindy Moyle is a Board Member, Fur Commission USA.

Harris Mink Farms (FF-M)
15258 Green Road
Caldwell, ID 83607
Phone: (208) 459-6015 or (208) 459-9359
Contact: Donald B. Harris, Scott L. Harris, Brent Harris
Notes: Very large mink farm. Scott Harris is Treasurer of Fur Commission USA (as of 2013).

Raft River Mink Ranch / Carson Farms (FF-M)
1174 S. Highway 81
Declo, ID 83323
Phone: (208) 645-3201
Contact: Nate & Desiree Carson

Kraemer Farm (FF-F)
RR1 Box 1065
Fairfield, ID 83327
Contact: Jim Kraemer

Moyle & Sons Fur Farm (FF-M)
(Rock Creek Canyon Ranch)
4052 North 2600 East
Filer, ID 83328
Phone: (208) 733-4440
Contact: Jay & Barbara Moyle, Dean
Moyle
Notes: Set back from road at end of
driveway.

Rock Ridge Farms (FF-M)
312 Parkinson Road
Franklin, ID 83237
Phone: (208) 646-2559
Contact: Todd & Natalie Hansen

Hobbs Fur Farm (FF-M) (FF-F)
331 Parkinson Road
Franklin, ID 83237
Phone: (208) 646-2418
Contact: Boyd T. Hobbs
Notes: Across the street from Kevin
Hobbs Fur Farm. Located on east side of
Parkinson & Little Mountain Roads.

Kevin Hobbs Fur Farm (FF-M) (FF-F)
4175 S. Parkinson Road
Franklin, ID 83237
Contact: Kevin Hobbs
Notes: Across the street from Hobbs Fur
Farm

Kingsford & Son (FF-M)
250 South 1st East
Franklin, ID 83237
Phone: (208) 646-2323
Contact: Larry Dean Kingsford

Whitehead Mink Ranch (FF-M)
205 South 2nd East
Franklin, ID 83237
Phone: (208) 646-2489
Contact: Jerry Whitehead
Notes: Very small farm. At far east end
of road. Sheds on N & S side of road.
Farm may be closed (investigation
needed).

Scot Hansen (FF-M)
244 South 2nd East
Franklin, ID 83237
Phone: (208) 760-0213
Notes: 3 sheds behind house on W side
of road. Directly east of Kingsford &
Son fur farm. Very small farm.

Fur farm (FF-M)
E end of E 100 N / Intersection of
Spring Creek Rd & Lowe Lane
Franklin, ID
Notes: Cluster of sheds N side of E 100
N / S side of Lowe Lane.

Roger Griffeth (FF-M)
38 W. Main
Franklin, ID 83237
Phone: (208) 646-2245
Notes: Across the street from a gas sta-
tion. Small farm.

Hobbs Furs (FF-M)
24 North 1st East
Franklin, ID 83237
Phone: (208) 646-2401
Contact: Jeffrey T. Hobbs
Notes: Also "pick your own" pumpkins
and squash. Very small farm.

Newbold Fur Farm (FF-M)
30 North 1st East
Franklin, ID 83237
Phone: (208) 646-2439, (208) 646-

2439
Contact: Eva Gene Newbold, Don
Newbold, Jr.
Notes: Very small farm.

Hawkes Fur Ranch (FF-M)
3647 East Maple Creek Road
Franklin, ID 83237
Phone: (208) 646-2423
Contact: Jerry Hawkes, David Hawkes

Brets Mink Ranch (FF-M)
2904 South 2800 East
Franklin, ID 83237
Phone: (208) 646-2513 or (208) 646-
2634
Contact: Bret D. & Annette Hansen
Notes: Located just south of E. Cub
River Road.

Mathews Brothers (FF-M)
670 Mingo Road
Grace, ID 83241
Phone: (208) 425-3351
Fax: (208) 425-3214
Contact: Mark D. Mathews, Dean
M. Mathews, Blair Mathews, Richard
Mathews

Moyle Mink Farm (FF-M)
390 South 600 West
Heyburn, ID 83336
Phone: (208) 678-8481
Contact: Lee & Martha Moyle
Notes: Large farm. Associated with
Moyle Mink and Tannery. East side of
road. 50 sheds. Visible from I-84. In
very commercial area.

Alpine Clean Food (FFFS)
374 South 600 West

Heyburn, ID 83336
Contact: Lee & Martha Moyle, Shannon
Wood
Notes: Fur farm feed supplier. At same
address, Moyle Mink & Tannery. Alpine
appears to be the in-house feed manufacturer of the Moyle Mink Company.
Unknown what other farms Alpine
supplies.

fur farm (FF-M)
460 South 850 West
Heyburn, ID 83336
Scott Harris and Donald Brent Harris,
managers

Ball Brothers Fur Farm / B&D Fur Farm
(FF-M)
2726 North 5600 West
Malad City, ID 83252
Contact: Bill & David Ball
Notes: The Ball brothers also operate a
fur farm in Morgan, Utah (B & D Fur
Farm). Large farm with 20,000 mink.
Updated address & farm name. Very re-
mote location. Approximately 24 sheds.
No house on site.

Smith Mink Farm (FF-M)
155 2nd Street West
Malta, ID 83342
Phone: (208) 645-2316
Contact: Cregg W. Smith, Carma Smith,
Osmer Smith
Notes: Located at end of service road
running W off of 2nd St, after bend. 11
sheds. Most sheds found empty. This
farm is very isolated and set back from
any travelled road. No house on site.
28,000 mink.

Moyle Mink Farm; Filer, Idaho

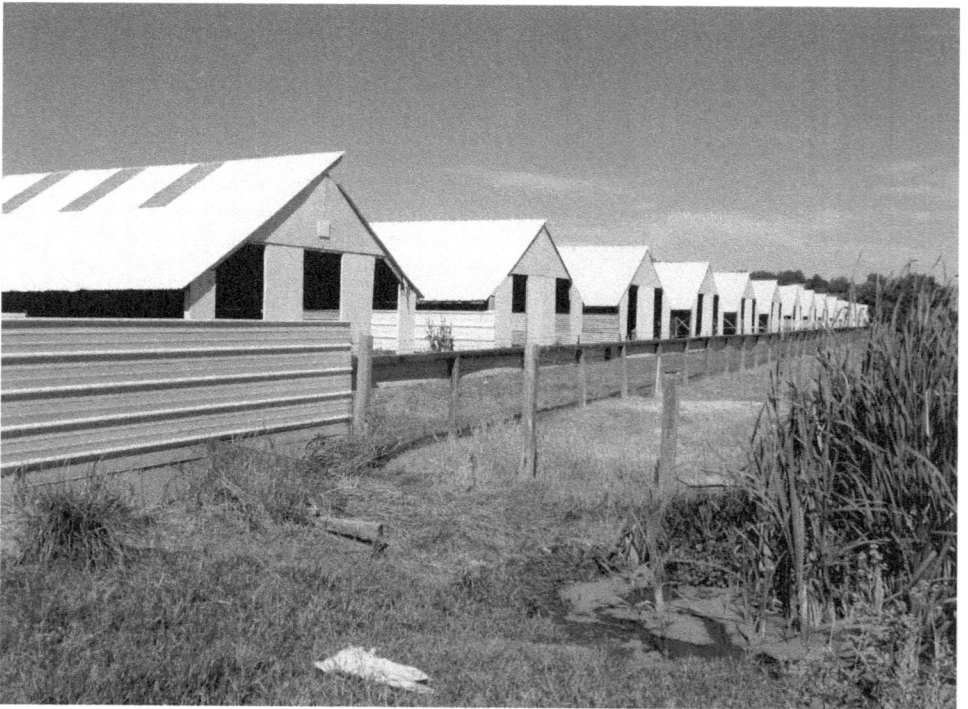

Moyle Mink Farm; Filer, Idaho

Geary Fur Farm; Burley, Idaho

Smith Mink Farm; Malta Idaho

Jack Rose, Professor of Physiology (FR)
Department of Biological Sciences
Idaho State University
Gale Life Sciences Bldg., Room 306/307
650 Memorial Drive
Pocatello, ID 83209
Phone: (208) 282-4261
Notes: Fur industry researcher. Received grants from Fur Commission USA (Mink Farmers Research Foundation) "to support his studies on delayed implantation in mink." Dr. Rose has received funding from the fur industry for many years to study reproduction in mink. Moyle Mink, also in Idaho, is supplying Jack Rose with animals. Address is for Rose's office. Location of mink unknown. Unconfirmed report his research on animals is done in the basement of the biology building.

Lew Palmer Mink Ranch (FF-M)
1768 South 600 West
Preston, ID 83263
Phone: (208) 852-1375
Contact: Lewis J. & Staci Palmer
Notes: Located across the street from Palmer Mink Farm.

Palmer Mink Ranch (FF-M) (FF-F)
1988 South 600 West
Preston, ID 83263
Contact: James R. & Linda Palmer
Notes: Sheds close to road. Located across the street from Lew Palmer Mink Farm.

Kent Griffeth Fur Farm (FF-M)
2214 S 1600 E
Preston, ID 83263
Phone: (208) 852-3118

Contact: Kent B. & Debbie Griffeth
Notes: Located at southwest corner of S 1600 E and E 2200 S.

Alder Fur Farm (FF-M)
1188 S 800 E
Preston, ID 83263

Griffin Fur Farm (FF-F) 440 West 800 South (440 W 8 S) Preston, ID 83263 Phone: (208) 852-2827 Contact: Keith Griffin, Kelly Griffin

Doney's Mink Ranch (FF-M)
753 E 3200 N
Preston, ID 83263
Phone: (208) 852-2178
Contact: Kay Doney

King Fur Ivien (FF-F)
118 Hangmans Road
Stites, ID 83552

CH Farm & Fur (FF-M) (FF-F)
22485 W 10500 S
Stone, ID 83252
Phone: (208) 705-7068
Contact: Corry & Hailey Hatch
Notes: Also wild fur buyer; receiving depot for North American Fur Auctions.

A-K Moyle Ranch (FF-M)
3539 South 1500 East
Wendell, ID 83355
Contact: Allen & Karla Moyle
Notes: Trail to the north of the sheds, along fence.

Sunny B Farms (FF-M)
2665 W 4400 S
Weston, ID 83286
Phone: (208) 747-3137
Contact: Kent W. & Suzanne R. Beckstead

Sandy Hill Mink Ranch (FF-M)
2951 West Hwy. 36
Weston, ID 83286
Contact: Dwain L. & Sandra Weeks
Notes: Unconfirmed. Evidence points
to active, 2009. No farm found at this
address, investigation needed.

Illinois

*Total mink imprisoned (2019 USDA
statistics): 109,000*

Avery Brabender (FF-M (FF-F)
27383 W Wilmot Road
Antioch, IL 60002
Phone: (847) 395-2782
Notes: Regularly advertises fox, mink
and pigeons for sale. Located south side
of road (farm not visible from road).

Littig Fox Farm (FF-F)
1774 Eagle Run Road
Bluffs, IL 62621
Phone: 217-754-3061, 217-754-3190
Contact: Kerry Littig, Terry Littig
Notes: Located at corner of Eagle Run
Road and Mueller Road. Terry Littig
is President of the U.S. Fox Shipper's
Council.

fur farm (FF-M)
Hunter Rd, east of Capron Rd
Capron IL 61012
Notes: Reportedly constructed in or
around 2015. Unconfirmed.

Johnson Farm (FF-F)
113 Whiteside
Columbia IL 62236
Contact: Eric Johnson

Frye's Fur Farm (FF-M)
2224 Behan Road
Crystal Lake, IL 60014
Phone: (815) 455-4862 or (815) 459-
0823
Contact: Larry Frye, Steve Frye, Robert
J. Frye
Notes: Large farm.

David Draves Fur & Archery (FF-F)
5758 N. 2200th Street
Dieterich, IL 62424
Contact: David W. Draves, Jessy Draves,
Victoria Draves
Notes: Farm may be closed (investiga-
tion needed).

MSC (formerly Milk Specialties Company) (FFFS)
260 S. Washington Street
Dundee, IL 60118
Phone: (800) 323-4274 or (847) 426-
3411
Contact: Trevor Tomkins, CEO
Notes: Owns National Feeds (largest fur
farm feed supplier, located in New Holstein, WI). Located at corner of Illinois
& Water Streets. Reported that no mink
feed is produced at this location.

Fox River Fur Farm (FF-M) (FF-F)
1498 N. 3975th Road
Earlville, IL 60518
Phone: (815) 792-8276 or (815) 792-
8501
Contact: Mark & Vicky Wiley
Notes: Mark Wiley is also President of
Freedom Sausage, a slaughterhouse in
Earlville. West of Chicago.

Montelone Mink Ranch (FF-M) (FF-F?)
43W891 Plato Road
Elgin, IL 60123

Phone: (847) 464-5118
Contact: Frank & Bernice Montelone
Notes: Large farm. Plato Road in Elgin is also known as County Road 32. May also be a fox farm. Plato Road in Elgin is also known as County Road 32.

Binkley Farm (FF-F)
13582W Springdale Road
Forreston IL 61030
Contact: Gretchen Binkley
Notes: Unconfirmed.

William Dumoulin (FF-M)
16N393 Walker Rd
Hampshire, IL 60140
Phone: (847) 683-3886
Notes Farm also has pigs and other animals. Satellite images how one long shed in rear of property, resembling a mink shed. Located on Walker Road between Allen Road and Highway 72.

fur farm (FF-M)
18113 Illinois Route 173
Harvard, IL 60033
Phone: (773) 497-5150
Contact: Jan & Maria Wolanin

Daniel Frey (FF-M)
26421 W. Molidor Road (at N. Fish Lake Road)
Ingleside (Volo), IL 60041
Notes: Farm reported closed (investigation needed).

Dawby Farm (FF-F)
503 E. Fairgrounds Ave.
Jerseyville IL 62052-2609
Contact: Emil Dawdy
Notes: Unconfirmed.

fur farm (FF-F)
17135 & 17141 Rosalind Street
Joliet, IL 60432
Contact: Robert L. & Joan C. Kern, and / or Richard Ross.
Notes: Confirmed open, 2010. Ross is a Catholic priest. Holds approximately 100 foxes. Cages at far south end of property, hidden in the woods.

Stahlheber Farm (FF-F)
Route 1 Box 312
Jonesboro IL 62952
Contact: Eric Stahlheber
Notes: Unconfirmed.

Gengel Mink Farm (FF-M)
38614 N. Fairfield Road
Lake Villa, IL 60046
Phone: (847) 356-5661
Contact: Ronald & Joanne Gengel
Notes: Ron Gengel is a Board Member, Fur Commission USA (as of 2014). The Gengel family also operates a Christmas tree farm (Gengel Tree Farm, in Lake Villa).

Illinois Mink Wire Company (FFES)
38614 N. Fairfield Road
Lake Villa, IL 60046
Phone: (800) 408-5661 or (847) 356-5661
Contact: Ron Gengel, Gerry Gengel
Notes: Sells Minkomatic feeders, fleshing/skinning machines and wire for cages. Illinois Mink Wire Co. is the U.S. representative for foreign fur farm suppliers, such as Dansk Mink Papir, Hedensted Gruppen, and Morsø Mink.

Matthew Richmiller (FF-F)
1213 E. 2000th Street
Liberty, IL 62347

Virgil Mink Ranch (FF-M)
48W310 Welter Road
Maple Park, IL 60151
Phone: (847) 365-6057
Contact: F.E. Geisen

Robert J. Diehl (FF-M)
46W500 Welter Road
Maple Park, IL 60151
Phone: (630) 365-6728

Hidden Farms (FF-M)
23707 Grange Road
Marengo, IL 60152
Contact: Roger Groenland
Notes: Farm may be closed (investiga-
tion needed).

Sorensen Mink Farm (FF-M)
19014 Kishwaukee Valley Road
Marengo, IL 60152
Contact: Hans Sorensen

East Fork Mink Ranch (FF-M)
1875 Nelson Road
Morris, IL 60450
Phone: (815) 942-1747
Contact: Robert & Brenda Rodeghero
Notes: Small farm.

Hall Farm (FF-F)
Route1 Box 161
Montrose IL 62445
Contact: Larry Hall
Notes: Unconfirmed.

Price Fox Farm (FF-M) (FF-F)
4850 Highway 141
Norris City, IL 62869
Phone: (618) 962-3284 or (618) 313-
2050
Contact: Clinton Price, Jr.

Lyle R. Reap (FF-F)
17828 W. Eagle Point Road
Polo, IL 61064
Phone: (815) 946-3702

Michael S. Singley Foxes (FF-F)
2792 S. Lincoln Avenue
Polo, IL 61064
Phone: (815) 946-3439
Notes: Farm may be closed (investiga-
tion needed).

Chenoweth Farms (FF-F)
4725 230th Street N
Port Byron, IL 61275
Phone: (309) 523-3773 or (309) 523-
2065
Contact: Ron & Denise Chenoweth
Notes: Located at the end of a long
drive, off of 230th Street. Farm may be
closed (investigation needed). Ron and
Denise also operate a dog boarding/
grooming business (Countryside Ken-
nel), and breed dogs and horses for sale.

Midwest Ingredients (FFFS)
103 West Main Street
Princeville, IL 61559
Phone: (309) 385-1035
Contact: Ruthi Coats

Fox Valley Foxes (FF-F)
2310 Bishop Road
Prophetstown IL 61277
815-537-5684
Contact: Michael Hunter
Notes: Unconfirmed.

Aeschleman Fur Company (FF-F)
1574 County Road 1600 East
Roanoke, IL 61561
Phone: (877) 266-6331, (309) 923-
7656
Contact: Daniel K. Aeschleman, Soni G.

Aeschleman
Notes: Also sells fox, deer, and raccoon urine to trappers.

Tim & Kim Allaman (FF-F)
1718 E State Highway 164
Rozetta, IL 61469
Notes: Also address for Fox Shippers Council.

Kaatz Bros. Lures (FF-F) (FF-MISC)
9986 Wacker Road
Savanna, IL 61074
Phone: (815) 273-2344
Contact: Kyle Kaatz, Kellen Kaatz
Notes: Fox farm and urine collection farm (ads claim that the urine is collected from wild, captive bobcats, coyotes, & foxes to create trapping lures), trapping supplies.

The Mink Barn (FF-M)
4609 Franklinville Road
Union, IL 60180
Contact: Vanessa Christensen
Notes: Farm reported closed in 2000 (investigation needed).

Imperial Mink Ranch (FF-M)
39495 N. Mill Creek Road
Wadsworth, IL 60083
Phone: (847) 336-6760
Contact: Jeff Serdar
Notes: Farm may be closed (investigation needed).

Indiana

Kindig Farm (FF-F)
7944 East 150 South
Akron IN, 46910
Contact: Gregory Kindig
Notes: Unconfirmed.

Griffith Farm (FF-F)
2161 North 700 East
Avilla IN 46710
Contact: Martin Griffiths
Notes: Unconfirmed.

Fur Information Council of America (FFO)
2611 16th Street
Bedford, IN 47421
(812) 797-4363
Principal officer: Andre Ferber
Notes: FICA provides background information and guidance on industry developments, researches markets trends and consumer habits, tracks and reports sales and price points, identifies issues of common concern, represents the fur industry in dealings with the press, the public sector and other industries, as well as state and federal governments. FICA monitors legislative initiatives and judicial actions that have direct impact on the fur industry.

Lakeview Fox Farm (FF-F)
9500 North Dearborn Road
Guilford IN 47022
812-623-2624
812-623-3386
Contact: Christopher & Tom McCann
Notes: Unconfirmed.

Rodenbeck Farm (FF-F)
720 Popular Street
Huntington IN 46750
Contact: Randy Rodenbeck
Notes: Unconfirmed.

Hidden Meadow Fur Farm (FF-F)
59821 County Rd 33
Middlebury, IN 46540
Phone: (219) 820-5930
Contact: Rick & Renea Miller

Lion Farms (FF-M)
9555 S 250 E
Nottingham (Keystone), IN 46759
Notes: Formerly a dairy farm. Lion Farms operates another mink farm a short distance away in Van Wert, Ohio.

Miller Farm (FF-F)
3294 540th St SW.
Riverside, IN 52327-9777
Contact: Rick Miller
Notes: Unconfirmed.

K & K Fur Producers (FF-F)
6739 N. Mayne Road
Roanoke, IN 46783
Contact: James L. Kahn, Thomas K. Kyle
Notes: Farm may be closed (investigation needed).

Flory Fur Farms (FF-F)
5440 State Road 110
Rochester, IN 46975
Contact: Doyle Flory
Notes: Farm may be closed (investigation needed).

Iowa

Total mink imprisoned (2019 USDA statistics): 129,000

Robert Roman (FF-F)
23778 Fairview Road
Anamosa, IA 52205
Phone: (319) 480-9107 or (319) 462-4107
Notes: Reportedly imprisons 300 fox.

Lyle Karels (FF-M)
3201 130th Avenue
Burt, IA 50522

Phone: (515) 924-3707

Perrin & Sons Fur Farm (FF-M) (FF-F)
1637 600th Street
Cherokee, IA 51012
Phone: (712) 225-5348
Contact: Kelly J. & Teri Perrin, C E Perrin
Notes: Large fur farm. Located west of Highway 59. N side of the road. Sheds directly on the road. Sheds & fox pens are at a great distance from the house. Dirt road. "Perrin Farm" sign posted.

Best Veterinary Solutions, Inc. (FFES)
1716 Detroit Street
Ellsworth, IA 50075
Phone: (888) 378-4045 or (515) 836-4001
Contact: Wes Thoreson, President
Notes: Supplies vaccines to fur farmers. Best Veterinary Solutions has distribution centers in Willmar, MN, Washington, IN, Dagsboro, DE and Manheim, PA.

Woodring Fur Farm (FF-M)
3020 250th Street
Fredericksburg, IA 50630
Phone: (563) 237-6523
Contact: Jean Woodring
Notes: Large fur farm. Located just west of Union Avenue/County Road V56. Sheds very close to the road. Dirt road.

Underwood Farm (FF-M)
2260 Quinlan Avenue
Fredericksburg, IA 50630
Contact: Justin Underwood, Mary J. Underwood
Notes: Located south of 220th Street, west of Roanoke Avenue. Many sheds have been removed from the property, some remain. Status unknown (investi-

Isebrands Fur Farm; Jewell, Iowa

Circle K Fur Farm; Sioux City, Iowa

Perrin & Sons Fur Farm; Cherokee, Iowa

Fasset Fur Farm; Webster City, Iowa

gation needed).

Hawkeye Mink Cooperative (FFFS)
1324 Main Street
Jewell, IA 50130
Phone: (515) 827-5458
Notes: Fur farm feed supplier & pelt
processor. Operational status unknown
(investigation needed).

Isebrands Fur Farm (FF-M)
3221 Queens Avenue
Jewell, IA 50130
Phone: (515) 827-5562
Contact: Mark Isebrands, Floyd L. &
Shirley Isebrands
Notes: Located between 320th and
330th Streets. Located between 320th
and 330th Streets. Open. Dirt road.
Many sheds directly on the road. House
at a significant distance from many of
the sheds.

Steve Hassebrock (FF-M)
Jewell, IA 50075
(515) 827-6198
Notes: Steve Hassebrock was a known
mink farmer at one point. Address of
farm, if it still exists, is unknown (investigation needed).

Don Conrad (FF-M) (FF-F)
1109 190th Street
Keota, IA 52248
Phone: (641) 636-3858
Notes: Located at southeast corner of
190th Street and Birch Avenue.

Gilbert C. Holmes (FF-M)
7510 Correctionville Rd.
Lawton, IA 51030
Phone: (712) 274-1285
Notes: Uninvestigated. Satellite images
show what may be mink sheds at this

location.

Paul Durkop (FF-F)
1429 185th Avenue
Lost Nation, IA 52254
Phone: (563) 678-2895 or (563) 219-
2835
Notes: Located south of 140th Street.

Schmuecker Fox Farm (FF-F)
7796 15th Avenue Trail
Luzerne, IA 52257
Contact: Dan Schmuecker
Notes: Located south of 77th Street
Drive.

Burgin Farm (FF-F)
1105 11th Street
Milford, IA 51351
Contact: Wesley Burgin
Notes: Unconfirmed.

fur farm (FF-M)
19075 County Road T14
Mystic, IA 52574
Phone: (641) 437-4028
Contact: Mark McGrann
Notes: Wide shed (4+ rows) behind
house. Address previously published as
19013 Highway T14. Mailboxes at end
of driveway read "19093" & "19075"
(two houses on driveway). Farm may be
closed (investigation needed).

Earl Drewelow & Sons (FF-M)
2477 239th Street
New Hampton, IA 50659
Notes: 239th St. is off Odessa Avenue,
north of 240th Street/County Road
B54. Earl Drewelow died February
2007; survived by his son Harvey. Best
viewed from 240th St. Numerous small
sheds and one large mink barn. Sheds at
a great distance from the house. Farmer

self-reported farm as closed. (Investigation needed). 14,000 mink.

Babcok Farm (FF-F)
1997 235th Street
New Hampton, IA 50659
Phone: 641-394-4927
Contact: Doug Babcock
Notes: Unconfirmed.

Ruby Fur Farm (FF-F)
2564 200th Street
New Sharon, IA 50207
Phone: (641) 672-2067
Contact: Randy Ruby, Mae Ruby
Notes: Also breeds ferrets, raccoons and skunks for the pet trade. "We specialize in breeding and raising ferrets, raccoons, and skunks and we offer them wholesale to pet stores." Dirt road. Two houses on property. Corn fields on all sides of sheds. Numerous species audible from inside farm.

North Star Fur Farm (FF-M)
26614 280th Street
Ollie, IA 52576
Phone: (641) 622-1001
Contact: Roger Warren
Notes: Small farm. S side of road. House in close proximity to sheds.

Silver Fox Farms (FF-F)
2596 370th Street
Osage, IA 50461
Contact: Brian Huffman
Notes: Small fox farm. Dirt road. Outdoor fox pens directly behind house.

Freeman's Fur and Feather (FF-F)
1381 380th Street
Osage, IA 50461
Phone: (641) 330-7864
Contact: Jeffrey J. Freeman

Klingbeil Mink Farm (FF-M)
22487 Tamarack Avenue
Remsen, IA 51050
Phone: (712) 786-3361
Contact: Donald Klingbeil
Notes: Large farm. Located between 220th and 230th Streets. West side of road. Farm is for sale (as of June 2012).

Elaine Doubek (FF-F)
3329 275th Street
Ridgeway, IA 52165

Morgan Valley Fox Farm (FF-F)
12420 S. 128th Avenue W.
Runnells, IA 50237
Phone: (515) 966-2028
Contact: Frank E. & Judy P. Rains
Notes: Located north side of road, just east of W. 125th Street S.

Bob & Julie Moran (FF-F)
3191 390th Avenue
Ruthven, IA 51358
Phone: (712) 859-3282 or (319) 480-9107

Dorothy & Allen Schwab (FF-F)
33714 280th St.
Shell Rock IA 50670
Phone: 319-987-2728
Notes: Also at this address, Fox Shippers/Fox Producers Council

Circle K Fur Farm (FF-M) (FF-F)
3701 Memorial Drive
Sioux City, IA 51104
Phone: (712) 252-2202
Contact: Steve Krage
Notes: Approximately 5,000 mink & 100 fox. Located north side of road. Sheds at a great distance from the house. Gate to rear of farm on Talbot, along

Hawkeye Mink Co-op; Jewel, Iowa

David Tremel; Woodbine, Iowa

Perrin & Sons; Cherokee, Iowa

Klingbeil Mink Farm; Remsen, Iowa

farm's W side.

Marak Fur Farm (FF-M) (FF-F)
1297 Marak Road NW
Swisher, IA 52338
Phone: (319) 857-4331
Contact: Darrel L. & Carolyn Marak
Notes: Darrel Marak also sells animal
urine. Farm on E side of road, house
& address on W side. At least one shed
visible from the road.

T & A Mink Farm (FF-M)
3209 240th Avenue
Titonka, IA 50480
Phone: (515) 928-2360
Contact: Tom & Amy Higgins

James M. Roberston (FF-F)
3794 Toddville Road
Toddville, IA 52341
Phone: (319) 393-4454
Contact: James M. & Florence Roberston
Notes: Heavily wooded property. S side
of road, up long driveway. Pens may be
located on the E side of the property, at
a distance from the house.

Andrews & Sons Fur Farm (FF-F)
32786 Highway D67
Union, IA 50258
Contact: Curt Andrews
Notes: Farm may be closed or at another
address.

Misty Moonlight Mink Ranch (FF-M)
1842 140th Street
Waverly, IA 50677
Phone: (319) 276-3350
Contact: Nick & Becky Demuth
Notes: Small farm. Sheds close to road,
on S side. House at a distance from
sheds.

Fassett Fur Farm (FF-M)
939 N. White Fox Road
Webster City, IA 50595
Phone: (515) 832-2094 or (515) 832-
5058
Contact: Jim F. Fassett, Tom Fassett
Notes: White Fox Road is also known as
R33. W side of Road. Sheds very close
to house.

Bush Farm (FF-F)
711 N 14th Ave
Winterset, IA 50273-1740
Contact: Dan Bush
Notes: Unconfirmed.

Shaw Farm (FF-F)
2250 Carver Road
Winterset IA 50273
Contact: John Shaw
Notes: Unconfirmed.

David Tremel (FF-M) (FF-F)
2017 Troy Trail
Woodbine, IA 51579
Phone: (712) 647-2191
Notes: Located west side of road,
approx. 1/2 mile south of 194th Street.
Service road cuts through field to the
north running directly behind farm,
parallel to 210th St.

Louisiana

Jones-Hamilton Co (FFFS)
428 Hidden Lake Court
Baton Rouge, LA
(225) 763-9990
Notes: Manufactures dry acid for mink
feed.

Massachusetts

Riverdale Mills Corporation (FFES)
130 Riverdale Street
Northbridge, MA 01534
Phone: (800) 762-6374 or (508) 234-8715
Contact: James M. Knott, Owner & CEO
Notes: Manufacturer of cages for mink farms.

Michigan

Total mink imprisoned (2019 USDA statistics): 80,000

Fox Haven (FF-F)
1806 E. Hinchman Road
Berrien Springs, MI 49103
Contact: James E. & Judith Brown

Lemon Creek Fox Ranch (FF-F)
2224 E. Lemon Creek Road
Berrien Springs, MI 49103
Contact: William V. & Norma Kechkaylo
Notes: At same address, Wicklewood Kennels.

Daniel Miller (FF-M)
23809 Truckenmiller Road
Centerville, MI 49032
Notes: Farm may be closed (investigation needed).

Robert Roell & Sons (FF-M)
N11218 State Highway 95
Channing, MI 49815
Contact: Robert Roell, Kenneth Roell, David Roell, Vince Roell
Notes: There are two large farms south of Channing on State Highway 95; east

side of road.

Brown Farm (FF-F)
253 Snuff Country Rd.
Crystal Falls, MI 49920-8627
Contact: Linda Brown
Notes: Unconfirmed.

Michigan State University Experimental Fur Farm (FR)
Steven J. Bursian, Ph.D.
Michigan State University
Department of Animal Science
5252 E Jolly Road.
East Lansing, MI 48824
Phone: (517) 355-8415
Fax: (517) 353-1699
Notes: Experimental fur farm. Also at this address: Poultry research farm. Bursian has received funding from the fur industry for many years. Dr. Bursian used to work with now-retired fur industry researcher Richard Aulerich. Farm reportedly on Jolly Rd between College Rd and Hagadorn Rd.

Sturdy Mink (FF-M)
5218 18.9 Lane
Gladstone, Ml 49837
Phone: (906) 786-7835
Contact: Robert & Rita Sturdy
Notes: Large farm. Entrance located off of 19th Lane, about 1/2 mile west of County Road 426/Michigan 5/G38.

Jander Fur Farm (FF-M)
N17725 County Road 551
Harris Township (Bark River), MI 49807
Phone: (906) 466-2909
Contact: Gregory Jander
Notes: Located at northwest corner of 551 and Dump Road Number 44.

Koski Farm (FF-F)
Route1 Box 235
L'Anse MI 49946
Contact: Dennis Koski
Notes: Unconfirmed.

Dale Hiatt (FF-F)
30985 Covey Road
Leonidas, MI 49066
Notes: Farm may be closed (investigation needed).

Sonnenberg Farm (FF-F)
2628 Stronach Road
Manistee MI 49660
Contact: Donald Sonnenberg
Notes: Unconfirmed.

Natural Fibers (FF-F)
17519 L Drive South
Marshall, MI 49068
Contact: Joe & Marie McFadden
Notes: Farm may be closed (investigation needed).

Geri Van Elderen (FF-M) 1540 6th
Street Martin, MI 49070 Phone: (269)
672-2115 Contact: Geri & Sheri Van
Elderen Notes: Farm may be closed
(investigation needed).
JET Mink Ranch (FF-M)
N2119 Bay De Noc Drive
Menominee, MI 49858
Phone: (906) 863-3113
Contact: John Kellogg
Notes: Large farm. Bay De Noc Drive is
also known as Old US 41. Farm is located at southwest corner of Bay De Noc
and 5.25 Lane, west of US 41.

Walcott Farm (FF-F)
7632 S Croswell
Newaygo MI 49337
Contact: Glen Walcott

Notes: Unconfirmed.

Robert W. Nesbit (FF-F)
5290 Sharp Road
Palmyra, MI 49268

Pipkorn, Inc. (FF-M)
W4503 US Highway 2
Powers, MI 49874
Phone: (906) 497-5725
Contact: Thomas D. Pipkorn, Steve
Pipkorn
Notes: Located between Kluba Lane and
Quarry Road K.5; south side of highway.
Two clusters of sheds, 1/2 block apart.
Second cluster at end of driveway, SE of
the house.

Greenway Farms (FF-F)
2928 Petersville Road
Rogers City, MI 49779
Contact: Marie E. Greenway

Bruning Mink and Fox Farm (FF-F)
2727 Klee Road
Rogers City MI 49779
Contact: Mark Bruning
Notes: Unconfirmed.

Fisk Fox Farm (FF-F)
11576 Sprague
Sand Lake, MI 49343
Phone: (616) 984-5564
Contact: Douglas R. and Diane Fisk

Van Elderen Brothers (FF-M)
2345 6th Street
Shelbyville, MI 49344
Phone: (269) 672-5123 or (616) 672-7390
Contact: Michael & Hermina Vanelderen
Notes: Van Elderen also operates a feed
mill in the nearby village of Martin (892

E. Allegan Street).

Bell Farm (FF-F)
235 30th Avenue
Six Lakes MI 48886
Contact: Larry Bell
Notes: Unconfirmed.

Scott & Amber McGee (FF-M)
E1751 Pantti Road
Skandia, MI 49885
Phone: (906) 439-5276
Notes: Small farm.

Kirchner Farm (FF-F)
677 S. Plymouth Rd.
Wakefield MI 49968-9522
Contact: Fred Kirchner
Notes: Unconfirmed.

LeFebre's Mink Farm (FF-M)
1260 146th Avenue
Wayland, Ml 49348
Contact: Randall J. LeFebre
Notes: Farm may be closed (investigation needed).

Scholten Fur Farm (Scholten Feeds)
(FF-M)
260 139th Avenue
Wayland, Ml 49348
Phone: (269) 792-7747
Contact: John Scholten
Notes: Large farm.

Roger Tourangeau III (FF-M)
N15072 D-1 Road
Wilson, MI 49896
Phone: (906) 466-2840
Notes: Farm may be closed (investigation needed).

Minnesota

Total mink imprisoned (2019 USDA statistics): 220,000

Tim Jahr (FF-F)
21496 401st Avenue
Arlington, MN 55307
Notes: Located south of 210th Street.
Thompson Farm (FF-F)
14283 160th Street South
Barneville, MN 56514
Phone: (612) 493-4460
Contact: Mike Thompson

Dusty Hough's Fur Shed (FF-F) (FF-MISC)
15432 90th Avenue South
Barnesville, MN 56514-9173
Phone: 218-937-5628
Notes: Fox, coyotes, beavers. Small urine collection operation. According to a report, the animals are imprisoned in small wire cages inside a building located at this address. Also a trapping supply operation, and the urine is sold as a trapping lures.

Big Falls Mink Ranch (FF-M)
8624 Highway 6
Big Falls, MN 56627
Phone: (218) 276-2467 or (218) 276-2357 or (218) 276-2429
Contact: Carl Larsen, Jeff Larsen, James Larsen
Notes: Located approx. 5 miles south of downtown Big Falls, on the Big Fork River.

North Central Fox Producers Association (FF-F)
26222 Co. Rd 318
Bovey MN 55709

Phone: 218-245-1175 or 218-263-7329
Contact: Thomas Tenney
Notes: Unconfirmed.

Eino Lake Fox Farm (FF-F)
21596 County Road 447
Bovey, MN 55709
-or-
374 Co. Rd. 447
Bovey MN 55709
Contact: Louis Baumel
Notes: Located on south side of road.
Both addresses appear to point to the
same property.

Fredrick Halvorson (FF-F)
39306 Highway 52
Cannon Falls, MN 55009

Whalen Foods Inc. (FFFS)
584 Bavaria Lane, Suite 200
Chaska, MN 55318
Phone: (866) 547-6510 or (952) 368-
6077
Notes: Supplies ingredients for mink
and fox feed; advertises in fur industry
publications.

Smokey Red's Snare Supply (FF-F)
11415 Salonen Road
Chisholm, MN
Notes: Advertising "fox pups for sale",
with contact number linked to the above
address. Uninvestigated.

Sharon Williams (FF-F)
3801 Jackson Road
Cloquet, MN 55720

Jergenson Mink Ranch (FF-M)
14747 380th Avenue
Cyrus, MN 56323
Phone: (320) 795-2487 or (320) 760-
0275

Contact: Duane Jergenson
Notes: Located north of 150th Street/
Township Road 144. West side of road.

Keith Sonnenberg (FF-M)
30786 State Highway 34
Detroit Lakes, MN 56501
Phone: (218) 847-5490
Notes: Located on north side of road.

fur farm (FF-M)
320th Avenue
Detroit Lakes, MN 56501
Notes: Located at end of road, entrance
off of State Highway 34.

Gill Gigstead (FF-M)
17296 County Road 29
Detroit Lakes, MN 56501
Phone: (218) 847-8059 or (218) 847-
7068
Contact: Gill Gigstead
Notes: Farm may be closed (investiga-
tion needed).

Bob's Mink Ranch (FF-M) (FFFS)
28603 State Highway 34
Detroit Lakes, MN 56501
Phone: (218) 847-8407 or (218) 846-
0933
Contact: Robert R. Sonnenberg
Notes: Large farm. Located east of De-
troit Lakes city center, north of highway.
At same address: Minnesota Fur Breed-
ers, and S & S Feed Company.

Castle - Lehmann, Inc. (FF-M)
41835 County Road 126
Detroit Lakes, MN 56501
Phone: (218) 847-5065
Contact: Gary L. Lehmann
Notes: Located between White Pine
Road and E. Long Lake Road; south side
of road.

Wayne A. Sieverding (FF-F)
36414 130th Street
Dundee, MN 56131
Phone: (507) 425-3205
Contact: Wayne & MaryAnn Sieverding
Notes: Located at the end of 130th
Street, on West Graham Lake.

Lang Farms (FF-M)
23588 County Road 34
Eden Valley, MN 55329

Urbach Farm (FF-M)
35693 State Highway 228
Frazee, MN 56544
Contact: Larry Urbach

Bennett Farm (FF-F)
34096 Co Hwy 4
Frazee MN 56544
Contact: Arnold Bennett
Notes: Unconfirmed.

Myhre Mink Ranch (FF-M)
75562 State Highway 16
Grand Meadow, MN 55936
Phone: (507) 754-5334
Contact: Einar Myhre

H & H Mink Ranch (FF-M)
Harmony MN 55939
Contact: James Haugerud
Notes: Address needed.

Kroschel Mink & Stock Farm (FF-M)
2937 330 Avenue
Hinckley, MN 55037
Phone: (320) 384-6976
Contact: Hugo & Fran Kroschel

Gary Klein Fur Farm (FF-M)
17827 Carnie Road
Hinckley, MN 55037

Phone: (320) 384-6688
Contact: Gary E. & Ann Klein
Notes: Located north side of road. Farm
may be closed (investigation needed).

Latzig Mink Ranch (Lakeside Ferrets)
(FF-M)
809 County Road 7 SW
Howard Lake, MN 55349
Phone: (320) 963-3594
Notes: Farm reported closed in 2011.
Unconfirmed. Located just north of
10th Street SW.

Vogt Fur Farm (FF-M)
205 (Donald)or 210 (John) Elm St.
Kasota, MN 56050
Phone: (507) 931-2829 or (507) 931-
3952
Contact: Donald & John Vogt
Notes: Located in NW corner of town,
between railroad tracks and Minnesota
River, at end of E. Elm Street. S

Mueller Bros. Mink Ranch (Mueller
Fleshing & Supply) (FF-M)
19086 County Road 141
Kimball, MN 55353
Phone: (320) 398-7787
Contact: James Mueller, Gregory Mueller
Notes: Large farm. Entrance located on
northwest shore of Pearl Lake.

Fur-Ever Wild (FF)
10132 235th Street W
Lakeville, MN 55044
Phone: (612) 467-9653
Contact: Terri Petter, Dan Storlie
Notes: Fur farm and roadside zoo.

Kavan Ranch (FF-M) (FF-F)
22802 Lexington Road
Le Center, MN 56057
Phone: (507) 357-4918

Contact: Tom Kavan, Jerry Kavan
Notes: Located north side of road, just east of 229th Avenue.

Terry Kimmet (FF-M)
21618 320th Street
Le Center, MN 56057
Notes: Farm may be closed (investigation needed).

Ballman Farm (FF-F)
25526 Dodd Road
Le Center MN 56057
Contact: Cease Ballman
Notes: Unconfirmed.

Litke Mink Ranch / J&S Mink (FF-M)
13472 Airport Road
Little Falls, MN 56345
Phone: (320) 632-6367
Contact: Gerald Litke
Notes: Located north of the Little Falls-Morrison County Airport; east side of road. At southeast corner of County Road 8 and Township 124, northeast of Luverne.

Ehde Brothers Fur Farm (FF-M)
County Road 8
Luverne, MN 56156
Phone: (507) 283-9747 or (507) 283-4771
Contact: Arthur Ehde
Notes: Located at southeast corner of County Road 8 and Township 124, northeast of Luverne.

Jeffrey Williams (FF-M)
10202 421st Avenue
Mabel, MN 55954
Phone: (507) 493-5049
Notes: Farm may be closed (investigation needed).

de Rosier, Inc. (FFFS)
412 South 4th Street, Suite 1153
Minneapolis, MN 55415
Phone: (612) 339-3566 or (612) 339-3599
Contact: John M. de Rosier
Notes: Supplies ingredients for mink feed; advertises in fur industry publications.

Garvin Brook Fox Ranch (FF-F)
Rural Route 1
Minnesota City, MN 55959
Notes: Address unknown.

North Central Companies (FFFS)
601 Carlson Parkway, Suite 400
Minnetonka, MN 55305
Phone: (952) 449-0885
Contact: Larry Zilverberg
Notes: Fur farm feed supplier.

Smieja Farm (FF-F)
2520 Eastwood Lane
Monticello MN 55362-9556
Contact: Scott Smieja
Notes: Unconfirmed.

Pomme De Terre Fur Farm (FF-M)
County Road 70
Morris, MN 56267
Phone: (320) 795-2729
Contact: Robert L. Jergenson
Notes: Located on County Road 70, approx. 1 mile east of US Highway 59, on the Pomme de Terre River.

Leslie R. Voges (FF-F)
1476 County Road 29
Nisswa, MN 56468
Phone: (218) 568 5560
Contact: Les & Jill Voges

Heger Company (FFFS)
2536 E. Seventh Avenue
North St. Paul, MN 55109
Phone: (800) 467-6465 or (651) 777-
3701
Contact: Dean Armstrong, Gregg 'Whi-
tie' Johnson
Notes: Fur farm feed supplier.

Richard Dorow Mink Farm (Custom
Fleshing Inc.) (FF-M)
31727 State Highway 108
Ottertail, MN 56571
Phone: (218) 367-2870
Contact: Richard & Gloria Dorow
Notes: Located on south side of road.

Kieffer Farm (FF-M) (FF-F)
6896 Partridge Road
Pierz, MN 56364
Phone: (320) 290-8722
Contact: Matthew Kieffer

Nature's Secret Fur Ranch (FF-F)
220 S Prairie Ave. #11
Porter MN 56280-3019
Douglas Merritt
Notes: Unconfirmed.

Lang's Mink Farm (FF-M)
19013 225th Street
Richmond, MN 56368
Phone: (320) 597-3400
Contact: John & Rosanne Lang

Coats of Many Colors Fox Ranch (FF-F)
37493 378th Street
Richville, MN 56576
Phone: (218) 758-2582
Contact: Jean Glass

Zumbro River Fur Farm (FF-M)
4625 West River Road NW

Rochester, MN 55901
Phone: (507) 529-8164 or (507) 282-
9665
Contact: Scott A. Stevens, Marian C.
Stevens, Larry N. Stevens.
Notes: West River Road NW is also
known as County Road 133.

Royal Oak Mink Ranch (FF-M)
20452 County Road 2
Sauk Centre, MN 56378
Phone: (320) 352-6866 or (320) 352-
6002
Contact: Steve Thang, Colleen Thang,
Jeff Thang
Notes: Located on north side of road, at
205th Avenue.

Saathoff Farm (FF-F)
588 140th Street
Sherburn MN 56171-1143
Contact: Charles Saathoff
Notes: Unconfirmed.

Ryan Fur Farm (FF-M)
21341 County 19
Spring Grove, MN 55974
Phone: (507) 498-3770 or (507) 429-
0070
Contact: Erin Ryan

Jarid Swenson (FF-F)
620 Warren Avenue
Spring Valley, MN 55975
Notes: Address may be incorrect (investigation needed).

Helickson Farm (FF-F)
RR 1 Box 1283
Spring Valley MN 55975-9790
Contact: Rusty Hellickson
Notes: Unconfirmed. Street address
needed.

Overend Farm (FF-F)
4096 105th Street SE
Stewartville MN 55976
Contact: Francis Overend
Notes: Unconfirmed.

Conlon's Silver Fox Farm (FF-F)
34807 382nd Street
St. Peter MN 56082
507-931-3716
Contact: Vince Conlon
Notes: Unconfirmed.

Gene Mosbeck (FF-F)
18284 110th Street NW
Thief River Falls, MN 56701
Phone: (218) 964-5360
Contact: Gene & Susan Mosbeck

Wenzel Soland (FF-M)
31247 County Highway 130
Vergas, MN 56587
Phone: (218) 342-2545
Notes: Located north side of road, just
west of 315th Avenue.

Schultz Fur Farm (FF-M)
31829 County Road 130
Vergas, MN 56587
Phone: (218) 342-2501
Contact: Arland & Karrie Schultz
Notes: Located north side of road, east
of 315th Avenue. One of the oldest fur
farms in the country, founded 1928.

Clear Creek Fox Farm (FF-F)
30244 County Highway 7
Wabasso (Seaforth), MN 56293
Contact: Ann Warner

North Country Furs & Taxidermy
(FF-F) (FF-MISC?)
66025 Kirkwood Dr.
Warroad MN 56763

Phone: 218-386-3479
Contact: Bill Boyd
Notes: May also imprisons bobcats.

Heinen Mink Ranch (FF-M)
33091 620th Street
Warroad, MN 56763
Phone: (218) 386-1194
Contact: George Heinen, Jr.
Notes: Located north of State Road 11.

Moeller Farm (FF-F)
RR1 Box 94
Welcome MN 56181
Contact: Jeff Moeller
Notes: Unconfirmed.

Neibuhr Farm (FF-F)
RR2 Box 129
Wells MN 56031
Contact: Rodney Neibuhr
Notes: Unconfirmed. Street address
needed.

Missouri

Spring Creek Fur Farm (FF)
24340 County Road 6420
Duke, MO
Notes: Address may be residence-only.
Investigation needed.

Woods Farm (FF-F)
Route 1 Box 51
Ellsinore MO 63937
Contact: Paul Woods
Notes: Unconfirmed. Street address
needed.

Mazuri / Purina Mills (FFFS)
100 Danforth Drive
Gray Summit, MO 63039
Phone: (800) 227-8941
Notes: Fox farm feed supplier. Mazuri is

Spotlight
Sky Halsey's Fox Farm, Martinsdale MT

Received anonymously.

"We entered Sky Haley's Silver Fox Ranch and are submitting the following info:

• The farm is open.
• There are approx. 6 rows of 15 pens, each housing one fox. This puts the approximate number of fox in outdoor pens at 100.
• There are three sheds to the west and north of the fox pens. Due to activity around the property, we were unable to determine the contents of the sheds. One or more of them is likely to hold horses (many horses were on the property).
• The fox pens are not in view of the house.
• The property is extremely difficult to access. From the front, all points of access were visible from the house (irrelevant for a nighttime visit). We hiked over two miles from the rear. Approaching proximity to the sheds, we traversed dense marsh, and even denser brush, before accessing the pens from the east.

Photos are being submitted with this report.

We would like to highlight to any future visitors of Sky Halsey's Silver Fox Ranch: The most difficult part is getting close to the property. Once you have made it to the pens, the rest of your visit – in whatever form it may take – will be a simple endeavor.

Anon"

Sky Halsey's Fox Farm; Martinsdale, Montana

Sky Halsey's Fox Farm; Martinsdale, Montana

Sky Halsey's Fox Farm; Martinsdale, Montana

Sky Halsey's Fox Farm; Martinsdale, Montana

the exotic animal brand of Purina Mills.

Mid-Missouri Fox Farm (FF-F)
12640 Derstler Road
Richmond, MO 64085
Contact: David W. Moyer
Notes: Located on west side of road,
north of railroad tracks.

Montana

Worbonnot (FF)
170 9th Ln NE
Fairfield, MT
Phone: (406) 467-2985
Status: Uninvestigated

Marshall & Nancy York (FF)
RR 1 Box 16a
Flaxville, MT
Phone: (406) 783-5388
Status: Uninvestigated. Street address
needed.

Dan Zieger (FF)
144 Sawney Drive
Glasgow, MT
Notes: Investigation needed. Address
may be a residence only.

Rocky Mountain Fur Company (FF-M)
(FF-F)
1477 US Hwy 93 South
Hamilton, MT 59840
Phone: (406) 363-6789
Contact: Dan J. Huggans
Notes: West side of highway. Set far back
from the road. Sheds at a distance from
the house.

Henke Mink Ranch (FF-M)
167 Antelope Creek Road
Hobson, MT 59452
Phone: (406) 423-5542

Contact: Richard & Darlene Henke
Notes: Located SW of town, approx. 2
miles SW of Ackley Lake. Very remote
location. Dirt road. Owners also breed
Akita dogs and operate trout fishing
ponds (Trophy Trout Springs Ranch).

Lee Buller (FF-MISC)
959 Riverside Road
Kalispell, MT 59901
Notes: Bobcat and lynx farm. Unknown
if animals are raised for fur or to be sold
as pets. Opened 2002. Farm raises "bobcat and lynx for personal and commercial purposes".

Pipe Creek Mink Ranch (FF-M)
5131 Pipe Creek Road
Libby, MT 59923
Phone: (406) 293-7582
Contact: Gary W. & Mary Ann Grenfell, Nick Grenfell
Notes: Located west side of road, just
north of Lodge Pole Way, approx. 6
miles north of city center.

Luke Jergenson (FF-M)
227 Pine Creek Road
Livingston, MT 59047
Phone: (406) 224-0729

Sky Dog Ranch / Sky Halsey's Silver Fox
Ranch (FF-F)
6913 US Highway 12 East
Martinsdale, MT 59053
Phone: (406) 572-3358
Contact: Sky & Eileen Halsey
Notes: Entrance on north side of road.
Over 100 black fox in free-standing
cages. North side of road. Set far back
from the road. Surrounded on two sides
by dense foliage and swampland.

Spotlight
Fraser Fur Farm

Received anonymously.

(The Fraser fur farm reportedly closed in 2017. The closure is unconfirmed.)

"In September, 2009, word circulated an investigation was sought for a major fur industry expose. The target: Fraser Fur Farm, largest wildcat farm in the country. North of Missoula, tucked off a small road east of downtown Ronan, are the cages that may imprison more lynx than exist in the wild in the entire state. Despite its significance, it is possible no one from the animal liberation movement had seen the inside of Fraser Fur Farm. The only recorded account of animal liberators getting close came in a brief mention in Strong Hearts, Rod Coronado's jailhouse zine. We set out for Ronan, MT, to verify the farm was open, confirm the species and numbers of animals, photograph the captives, map the farm's layout, and release the info to the public.

While most fur farms are easily accessed, Fraser's was an exception. It was immediately clear why help was being sought – this was one of the few farms not visible from the road, unable to be investigated without breaching property lines, and once inside: incredibly difficult to gain access to animals without being in view of a house.

A pre-investigation nighttime visit found the farm sat at the end of a dirt driveway off Terrace Lake Rd. The first visit we stayed to the distant perimeter, familiarizing ourselves with the layout. The outline of cages and rattle of large animals hinted at what lay in the shadows, just out of sight. This level of preparation was necessary because to obtain the documentation we sought, a nighttime visit was insufficient. We would have to access the farm mid-day.

The next morning we parked in a residential neighborhood off Timberlane Road, at what we approximated was a point one mile due south of the farm. Our nighttime survey had found two houses on site, making unsafe any attempt at approaching from the front.

Gunshots of hunter's echoed in the forest around us, and we entered the woods. In short time we found the faint outline of a trail, following it along a fence for one mile until we came into a clearing. Our shot-in-the-dark calculation had bore fruit: we were precisely at the rear of the Fraser Fur Farm.

At the only sliver of an angle not visible to either house, we emerged from the forest at the end of a long shed. We were met with the stare of a large, caged lynx. As majestic as imagined, the lynx seemed to have fallen through the cracks of time, pacing endlessly in its cage, waiting for the freedom just out of its reach. We were now two of the only people in the U.S. to ever lay eyes on a live lynx.

We surveyed four sheds and one long row of lynx pens. Available information put the animals held at Fraser as mink, bobcats, and lynx.

Four shed housing mink were found to be empty, and it is possible the farm no longer imprisons mink. We were unable to confirm the presence of bobcats, but many sheds were not inspected. One long row of pens held approximately 50 lynx; possibly more than exist in the wild.

We heavily documented the farm on video and with still photos. The documentation was submitted anonymously to aboveground contacts. We hope they will make these images – which may be the only existing photos of captive U.S. lynx – available to the public.

A final word on this farm: There would be no easy replacement – if any at all – for lost lynx breeding stock. More than any other animal raised for fur, the loss of irreplaceable lynx breeding stock would very likely be the end of this farm, and perhaps lynx farming in the U.S. Lastly, the person to liberate the captives of Fraser Fur Farm will have one historic accomplishment to their credit: possibly doubling the wild lynx population in Montana.

Thousands of us. Only one Fraser Fur Farm. Do the math.

Anonymous"

Frazier Fur Farm (FF-MISC)
6934 Highway 200
-or-
661 Highway 200 West
Plains, MT 59859
Phone: (406) 826-3151 or (406) 544-1487
Contact: Shelli Frazier
Notes: Bobcat farm; Shelli Frazier also sells horses. Opened 2006. "When fully operational, operators have indicated that they may have up to 50 bobcats on the premises". Unclear if purpose is for fur or pets.

Fraser Fur Farm (FF-F) (FF-MISC)
1348 Terrace Lake Road
Ronan, MT 59864
Phone: (406) 676-3177
Contact: Corey & Kathy Richwine
Notes: May be closed. Fox, bobcat, lynx farm. Farm also sells animal urine. Located east of downtown Ronan, south side of road. The Richwine family operate the Burgerville restaurant in Polson, MT. Reportedly one of only two large scale cat farms in the US. Auction records show Corey Richwine sold the following in one auction: Coyotes: 43, red fox: 9, cross fox: 2, bobcats: 87. Unclear if all animals were farmed, or some live-trapped. There is talk in the fur industry that this farm closed in 2018. Investigation needed.

Schultz Fur Farm (FF-MISC)
5700 Romunstad Road
Roy, MT 59471
Phone: (701) 570-6964
Contact: Larry Schultz, Carol Bomstad
Notes: Bobcat & lynx farm (under construction). In October 2014, Schultz was issued a license by Montana Fish,

Wildlife & Parks to move his fur farm from North Dakota to Montana. Media reports name this as one of only two large scale cat farms in the US (the other is likely to be Fraser Fur Farm in Ronan, MT).

Campbell's Mink Ranch (FF-M)
845 Southside Road
Superior, MT 59872
Phone: (406) 822-4448
Contact: David Campbell, Buddy Campbell, Dale Campbell
Notes: South side of road, just west of I-90. First driveway on left after bend, when Southside Road crosses under I-90 going from north to south.

David Thompson (FF-MISC)
Little Wolf Creek Road (Coordinates: T15N R5W NW1/4 S4)
Wolf Creek, MT 59648
Notes: Bobcat and lynx farm. Unknown if animals are raised for fur or to be sold as pets.

Nebraska

Fesler Fur Farm (FF-M)
Colon, NE
Phone: (402) 647-2755
Contact: Jack L. Fesler
Status: Uninvestigated.

Smeal Hide & Fur (FF-F)
710 Spruce Street
North Bend NE 68649-3507
Notes: Unconfirmed.

BHJ USA (FFFS)
2510 Ed Babe Gomez Avenue
Omaha, NE 68107
Phone: (402) 734-8030
Notes: Fur farm feed supplier.

Fraser Fur Farm; Ronan, Montana

Fraser Fur Farm; Ronan, Montana

Fraser Fur Farm; Ronan, Montana

Fraser Fur Farm; Ronan, Montana

John & Peggy Smeal (FF-F) (FFFS)
963 County Road F
Scribner, NE 68057
Phone: (402) 664-3362
Notes: Located between CR-9 and CR-10. At same address, Heartland Blends (fur farm feed supplier). Fox housed in indoor sheds. Dirt road runs from CR-F to the sheds. John Schmiel, President, North Central Fox Producers Assn.

New Hampshire

Richard Gauthier (FF-M) (FF-F)
845 Center Road
Lyndeborough, NH 03082
Phone: (603) 654-2904
Contact: Richard & Patricia Gauthier

New York

Pachucinski Farm (FF-F)
2733 Lenox Road
Collins, NY 14034
Phone: (716) 276-2311
Contact: Alfred J. Pachucinski, Jr.

Silver Ridge Ranch (FF-F)
1143 Garfield Road
East Nassau NY 12062
Phone: 518-733-6544
Contact: Tim Donohue
Notes: Unconfirmed.

Sutter Farm (FF-F)
PO Box 502
Grand Island NY 14072-0502
Contact: Michael Sutter
Notes: Unconfirmed

Conte Farm (FF-F)
3383 State Route 28
Herkimer NY 13350
Contact: John Conte
Notes: Unconfirmed.

Butternut Creek Mink Ranch (FF-M)
1428 East Side Road
Morris, NY 13808
Phone: (607) 263-2094
Contact: Robert Przekop
Notes: Farm located at southwest corner of East Side/River Road and County Road 51.

The American Fur Merchants Association (FFO)
224 West 30th Street, Suite 705
New York, NY 10001
Phone: (212) 564-5133
Contact: Steve Mechutan, President; Allen Soifer, Vice President; Helmut Rothe, Treasurer
Notes: At same address: Fur Merchants Employers Council

Johnson Farm (FF-F)
23 E. Main St.
Panama NY 14757-9730
Contact: Betty Johnson
Notes: Unconfirmed.

Phillips Fur Farm (FF-M)
59 Biddlecum Road
Pennelville, NY 13132
Phone: (315) 695-2401
Contact: Joseph & Releen Phillips
Notes: Farm may be closed (investigation needed).

Callan Farm (FF-F)
807 Hill Avenue
Pinebush NY 12566
Contact: John Callan
Notes: Unconfirmed.

Pelton Fur Farm (FF-M)
5046 Rome Taberg Road (State Route 69)
Rome, NY 13440
Phone: (315) 336-2619
Contact: Douglas & Joanne Pelton
Notes: Small farm located about 1/4 mile south of Humaston Road, on the southwest side of the road.

Bennett Fur Farm (FF-M)
Bennett Road (1939 Bennett Road?)
Victor, NY 14564
Contact: Roger Bennett
Notes: Large farm. Located on both sides of Bennett Road, between County Road 39 and Strong Road.

fur farm (FF-M)
County Road 64, south of the intersection of Bennett Road & CR 64
Victor, NY 14564
Notes: Located just south of the Bennett Fur Farm.

Liberty Fur Farms (FF-M)
County Route 53
Winthrop, NY 13697
(Alternate address: 319 Finnegan Road, Brasher Falls, NY 13613)
Phone: (315) 389-5700
Contact: Thomas J. & Helen Liberty

North Dakota

North Central Fox Producer's Association (FF-F?)
7545 Highway 2
Devil's Lake ND 58301
Contact: Mike Liane
Notes: Possible fox farm. The organiza-tion exists "to educate fox farmers and promote fur industry, fox farming."

Haroldson Farm (FF-F)
401 Erickson Street
Coteau ND 58721
Contact: Chris Haroldson
Notes: Unconfirmed.

Roy M. Kringstad (FF-F)
7516 County Road 4
Drayton, ND 58225

Schmit Farm (FF-F)
RR2 Box 131
Kenmore ND 58746
Contact: Michael Schmit
Notes: Unconfirmed. Street address needed.

Louis Wohlwend (FF-F)
9590 150th Avenue SE
Lidgerwood, ND 58053
Notes: Farm may be closed (investiga-tion needed).

Ohio

Jorney Mink Ranch (FF-M)
22199 Center Road
Alliance, OH 44601
Phone: (330) 525-7655
Contact: George Jorney, Justine Jorney
Notes: Located on the south side of road, between S. Mahoning Avenue and Homeworth Road/401.

Circle R Fox Ranch (FF-F)
1895 Riggle Road
Bellville, OH 44813
Phone: (419) 892-2445
Contact: William B. Ridenour
Notes: Located just east of CR-379.

Mark Hofacre (FF-M)
5661 Massillon Road
Dalton, OH 44618
Phone: (330) 837-2037
Notes: Farm is located on a dirt road off
of/to the southeast of Massillon Road/
State Route 241.

Blosser Farm (FF-F)
18470 Buckskin Road
Defiance OH 43512
Contact: Joe Blosser
Notes: Unconfirmed.

Schmitt Fur Farm (FF-M)
1038 State Route 119
Fort Recovery, OH 45846
Phone: (419) 375-4192
Contact: David Schmitt
Notes: Very large farm. Located just
east of downtown Fort Recovery, on the
south/east side of road. Said to be one of
the oldest mink farms still operating in
the U.S.

Kinsley Farm (FF-F)
3605 US Route 50 West
Hillsboro OH 45133
Contact: Albert Kinsley
Notes: Unconfirmed.

Silver Gates Fur Farm (FF-M)
17822 Township Road 104
Kenton, OH 43326
Contact: Kim Auger
Notes: Farm may be closed (confirma-
tion needed).

Tonn's Mink Farm (FF-M)
3270 Pigeon Run Road SW
Massillon, OH 44647
Phone: (330) 833-4972
Contact: Dennis & Wanda Tonn

Notes: Located on the east side of road,
just north of State Road 30.

Bering Farm (FF-F)
13960 Boyd Road
Mt. Orob OH 45154
Contact: Mark Bering
Notes: Unconfirmed.

Buschur Feeds (FFFS)
14417 Johnson Road
New Weston, OH 45348
Phone: (419) 925-5050 or (419) 305-
8277
Contact: Edward Buschur, President
Notes: Owns National Feeds (fur farm
feed supplier); see National Feeds (New
Holstein, WI).

Bekaert Corporation (FFES)
322 East Pine Street
Orrville, OH 44667
Phone: (330) 683-5060
Notes: Among this company's many
steel-wire products, Bekaert manufactures Weldmesh mink cages. Manufacturing plants also in Van Buren, AR and
Shelbyville, KY.

Grand River Fur Exchange (FF-F)
6310 US Highway 6
Rome, OH 44085
Phone: (440) 474-8678
Contact: Mark Gutman
Notes: Fox farm, urine farm (urine is
collected from captive coyotes and foxes
to create trapping lures). Wild fur buyer.
Located west of Hyde Road.

Lion Farms (FF-M)
2707 Hoaglin Rd
Van Wert, Ohio. 45891
Notes: Owned by a mink farmer from
Holland, who owns several other farms.

He employs a local farmer to operate this farm. Address appears to be registered to "Lion Farms," also the owner of a nearby mink farm in Nottingham, Indiana. On the Indiana border.

Jones-Hamilton Co.
30354 Tracy Road
Walbridge, OH 43465
Phone: (888) 858-4425
Notes: Produces Sodium Bisulfate acidifier for use in mink feed; advertises in fur industry publications.

B.J. Hoffman (FF-M)
3198 Crater
Wooster, OH 44691
Phone: (330) 345-7837

Oregon

Total number of mink imprisoned (2019 USDA statistics): 315,000

Autio Company (FFES)
93750 Autio Loop
Astoria, OR
Phone: (503) 458-6191
Notes: Fur farm equipment supplier. Sells grinders, mixers, and electric feed carts.

Stunkard Farm (FF-M)
41653 Old Hwy. 30
Astoria, OR 97103
Phone: (503) 458-6332
Contact: Marvin W. & Susan E. Stunkard, Matthew Stunkard
Notes: 8,400 mink.

Western Star Fur Farm (FF-M)
40801 Savola Lane
Astoria, OR 97103
Phone: (503) 522-7805 or (503) 458-

5167
Contact: Carl & Patricia Salo
Notes: Located on east side of road, north of School House Road.

Glade Wilkinson (FF-M) (FFFS)
36089 Binder Slough Lane
Astoria, OR 97103
Phone: (503) 338-6848
Notes: This address is listed as the Oregon feed production site for Northwest Farm Feed. Located east of Youngs River Road, on the water. House at a distance from the sheds.

Weisdorfer Fur Farm (FF-M)
11330 SE 272 Avenue
Boring, OR 97009
Phone: (503) 663-3070
Contact: Leo D. & Dawn Y. Weisdorfer
Notes: Located at corner of SE 272nd Avenue and SE Haley Road. Very large sheds with dozens of rows each. Farm is most visible via a bike path running along farm's W side.

Higgins New Horizon Farm (FF?)
5162 Sams Valley Rd
Gold Hill, OR 97525-9624
Notes: Uninvestigated. Listed as "agave production and fur farming." Species unknown.

Kropf Feed (FFFS)
815 S 2nd St
Harrisburg OR 97446
Notes: Possible fur farm feed supplier. Appears to have a connection to the fur industry, however this company's exact role is unknown. Investigation needed.

Jefferson Fur Farm (FF-M)
1477 Talbot Road SE
Jefferson, OR 97352

Arritola Mink Ranch; Mount Angel, Oregon

Krull, Masog, & Slack mink farms; Lebanon, Oregon

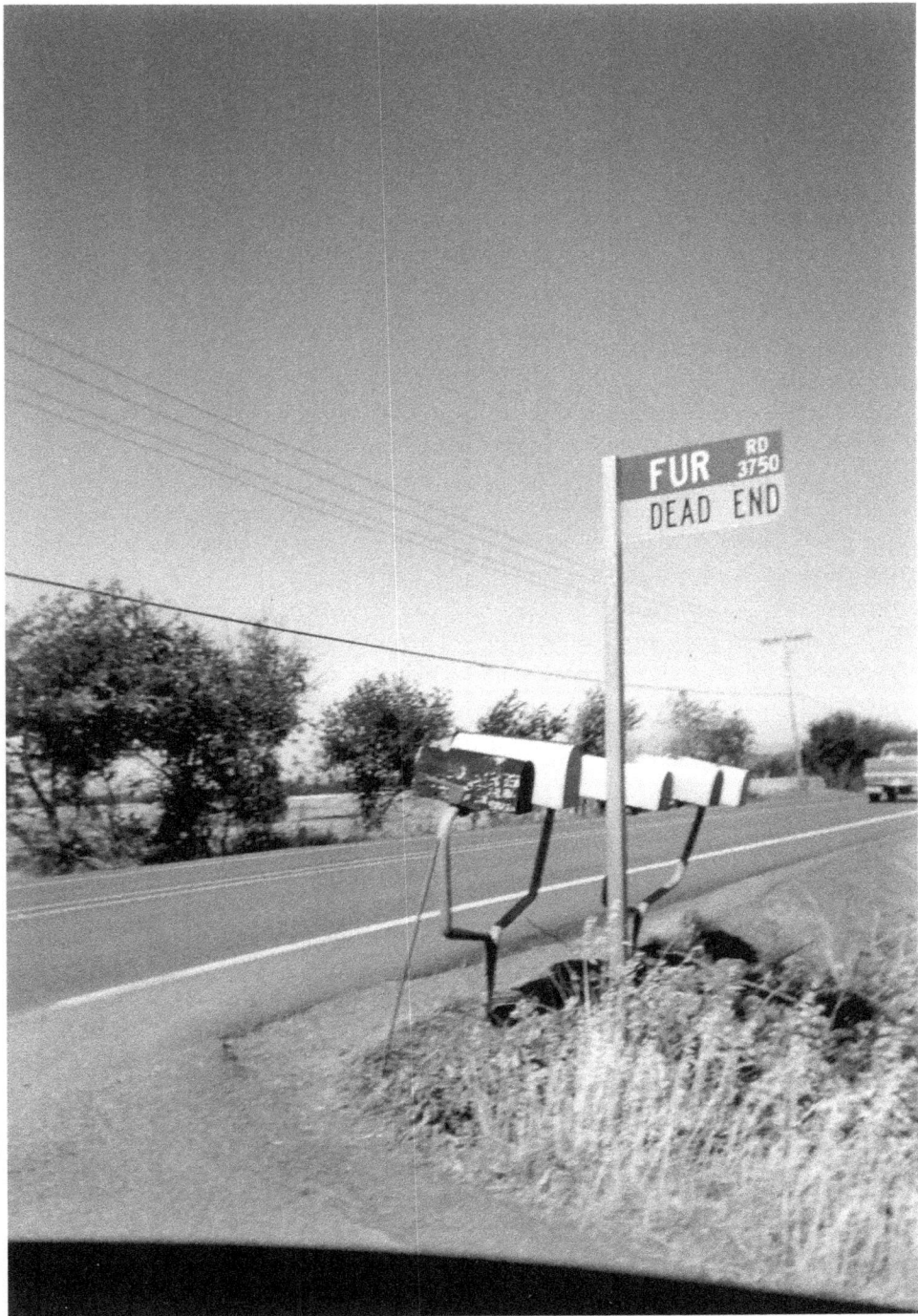

Phone: (541) 327-2275 or (541) 327-2420
Contact: Michael J. Posch, Joseph E. Posch,
Michael P. Posch, James F. Posch, Daniel S. Posch, Mary Posch
Notes: Small farm. Located on east side of road, north of Miller Road SE. Best vantage point from White Lane. White mink.

E.H. Webster (FF-M) (FF-F?)
Approximately 1059 2nd St
Jefferson, OR
Notes: Farm previously published as a fox farm. Only mink seen on investigation. Located on east side of road. Another entrance off of Jefferson-Marion Road (2750 Jefferson-Marion Road SE). Street numbers are approximate.

The following three farms are located on the same property, west of the Lebanon airport:

Arnold Krull (FF-M)
32564 Fur Rd.
Lebanon, OR
(541) 258-2510
Arnold L. & Leo J. Krull

Slack Farms (FF-M)
32600 Fur Road
Lebanon, OR 97355
Phone: (541) 258-2495
Contact: Richard & Dannette Slack, Dale Slack, Leroy Slack

Masog Mink Ranch (FF-M)
36232 W. Oak Street
Lebanon, OR 97355
Phone: (541) 619-3665 or (541) 259-3751
Contact: Lou & Kimberly Masog, Du-ane & Berlita Masog

McDowell Creek Mink Ranch (FF-M)
40283 McDowell Creek Dr
Lebanon, OR 97355
Contact: Russell, Duane and Louis Masog

Richard Graham (FF-M)
34481 Cottonwood Lane
Lebanon, OR 97355
Phone: (541) 258-5749

Fur Commission USA (FFO)
PO Box 1532
Medford, OR 97501
Phone: (541) 595-8568
Fax: (541) 566-7489
Web: www.furcommission.com, furresearch.org
Contact: Michael Whelan, Executive Director; Barbara Whelan, Executive Assistant
Notes: Fur Commission USA is a trade association representing American mink farmers. The majority of its funding comes from pelt assessments collected at North American Fur Auctions, and grants by the International Fur Trade Federation.
Board of Directors (as of 2017): Ron Gengel, President; Kolby Stembridge, Vice President; Scott Harris, Treasurer; Mark Stahl, Secretary; Ryan Holt, Board member; Clayton Beckstead, Board member; Robert Zimbal, Board member; Dr. John Easley, Board member; Michael Whelan, Executive Director.

Arritola Mink Ranch (FF-M)
12303 Mt Angel Gervais Road
Mount Angel, OR 97362
Phone: (503) 845-6272
Contact: Richard E. & Charlene L. Arri-

tola, Lance C. & Jodi L. Arritola
Notes: Heavily fortified. Tall razor wire fence, spotlights, and second fence inside first. Set far back from road. On railroad tracks. Sheds NE of farm are greenhouses.

Clem Ruef & Sons (also known as Oregon Mink / Ormink) (FF-M)
11658 Baron Road NE
Mount Angel, OR 97362
Phone: (503) 845-2800
Contact: Clement J. Ruef, Robert W. Ruef, Donald F. Ruef
Notes: Located just north of Arritola Mink Ranch. Also heavily fortified. Best viewed via railroad tracks on E side. Mink farm and fur farm feed supplier.

Ruef's Fur Ranch (FF-M)
12305 Reuf Lane
Mount Angel, OR 97362
Phone: (503) 845-2589 or (503) 845-6565 or (503) 845-6180
Contact: Max J. & Marlene Ruef, Joe & Darcy Ruef
Notes: Located off of W. Church Road NE. Sheds are controlled-environment sheds, walled-off on all sides. Cornfield service road runs along south of farm, from near the golf course. Farm is barely visible from the road.

Garten Services (FFES)
3334 Industrial Way NE
Salem, OR 97301
Phone: (503) 581-4472
Contact: Steven Elmore
Notes: Manufactures bedding material for mink farms; advertises in fur industry publications.

Delany's Fur Ranch (FF-M)
21318 Hazelnut Ridge Road
Scotts Mills, OR 97375
Phone: (503) 873-2005
Contact: David Delany, Judy Kandi

Black & Blue Farms (FF-M) (FF-F)
17621 Fern Ridge Road SE
Stayton, OR 97383
Phone: (503) 769-2575 or (503) 769-1481
Contact: Terry W. & Lyndia J. Basl
Notes: Lyndia is the owner of a local convenience store, Detroit Market (100 Detroit Ave. N., Detroit, Oregon).

Gardner Fur Farm (FF-F) (FF-M?)
3701 Drift Creek Rd SE
Sublimity, OR 97385
Phone: (503) 873-8405 or (503) 767-2845
Contact: Tim & Katie Gardner, Larry Gardner
Notes: Large fox farm. Located on west side of road, set far back from road. House is at a great distance from the sheds.

Undiscovered mink farm (FF-M?)
Sublimity, Oregon
Notes: A leaked security alert from the Fur Commission USA described a suspicious vehicle seen near a mink farm outside Sublimity. The only known fur farm in or around Sublimity is the Gardner Fur Farm. This information raises the possibility either the Gardner farm imprisons mink, or there is another undiscovered mink farm nearby.

Cascade Farms of Oregon (FF-M)
7582 Hunsaker Road SE
Turner, OR 97392
Phone: (503) 743-4295
Contact: John Lucas, Donna Lucas, Randy Lucas

Pennsylvania

Total number of mink imprisoned (2019 USDA statistics): 95,000

Scintilla Development Company / Avecon Diagnostics (FR)
501 Grouse Drive
Bath, PA 18014
Contact: Robert L. Stephon
Notes: Provides disease (Aleutian Disease Virus) testing for mink farmers. Scintilla Development Company received a $3,000 grant in 2007 from the Fur Commission USA. Reportedly performs its research at the Michigan State University experimental fur farm.

Oakwood Mink Farm (FF-M)
108 Oakwood Road
Boyers, PA 16020
Phone: (724) 735-2175
Contact: Robert & Kim DeMatteis

Bogus Fur Farm (FF-M)
360 Theatre Road
Carrolltown, PA 15722
Phone: (814) 344-6651
Contact: James & Rosalie Bogus

Mitchell Farm (FF-F)
RR3 Box 84
Clearfield PA 16830
Contact: Richard Mitchell
Notes: Unconfirmed. Street address needed.

Gerhard Bilek (FF-F)
9225 Fillinger Road
Cranesville PA 16410
Notes: Unconfirmed.

Glen Trone (FF-F)
400 Hess Farm Road

Dallastown, PA 17313
Notes: Farm may be closed (investigation needed).

Staples Farm (FF-F)
RR3 Box 3201
East Stroudburg PA 18301
Contact: Rick Staples
Notes: Unconfirmed. Street address needed.

Watcher Farm (FF-F)
246 Municipal Road
Ebensburg PA 15931
Contact: Dennis Watcher
Notes: Unconfirmed.

George Rykola (FF-M)
557 Colver Road
Ebensburg, PA 15931
Phone: (814) 472-8447

Western Pennsylvania Fur Farmers Cooperative Association (FFFS)
1401 Lemon Drop Road
Ebensburg, PA 15931
Phone: (814) 674-8069
Jim Bogus, President/General Manager (814-886-8948)
Notes: Fur farm feed supplier. Located at southwest corner of Lemon Drop and Brick Roads.

Mindek Brothers Fur Farm (FF-M)
4940 Shannon Road, 4937 Shannon Road
Erie, PA 16510
Phone: (814) 825-5047 or (814) 825-5310
Contact: Forrest J. Mindek, Nick O. Mindek, Hunter L. Mindek

Lawrence Dana Fox Ranch (FF-F)
9129 Station Road

Erie, PA 16510
Phone: (814) 725-1669

Preston Fur Farm (FF-M)
383 S. Good Hope Road
Greenville, PA 16125
Phone: (724) 588-5374 or (724) 588-7973
Contact: James L. Preston, Gary Preston, Gail & Lorri Preston

Priselac Farm (FF-F)
5437 Green Acres Road
Houtzdale, PA 16651
Contact: Joseph Priselac
Notes: Also a dairy farm.

Egolf Farm (FF-F)
444 North Lane
Mahaffey PA 15757
Contact: Charles Egolf Jr.
Notes: Unconfirmed.

Zullinger Farm (FF-F)
RD1 Box 178
Millerstown PA 17062
Contact: Rodney Zullinger
Notes: Unconfirmed. Street address needed.

George Holtzapple (FF-M)
6206 New Columbia Road
New Columbia, PA 17856
Phone: (717) 524-2079
Notes: Farm may be closed (investigation needed).

Kuzar (FF-M)
109 Mink Farm Lane
Nicktown, PA 15762
Phone: (814) 948-5614
Contact: Steve & Doris Kuzar

Fluharty Furs (FF-M)
526 Schultz Road
Perkiomenville, PA 18074
Phone: (610) 754-6781 or (610) 754-6162
Contact: Scott Fluharty
Notes: Farm is located to the east of Schultz Road, hidden in trees.

Caruso Farm (FF-F)
Box 67
Roscoe PA 15477
Contact: Al Caruso
Notes: Unconfirmed. Street address needed.

Richard H. Stahl & Sons Fur Farm (FF-M)
275 Fegley Road
Sunbury, PA 17801
Phone: (570) 286-2157 or (570) 286-2262
Contact: Mark Stahl, Rick Stahl, Alma Stahl
Notes: Fegley Road runs parallel to State Route 890, southeast of the City of Sunbury. Farm located east side of road. Spent $207,500 on "construction, renovations, security upgrades and new machinery and equipment" in 2009.

Goose Hill Fur Farm (FF-M)
Goose Hill Road
Wyalusing, PA 18853
Notes: Located on east side of road (set far back), south of Jenning Road.

South Dakota

Milo Pfeiffer (FF-F)
12998 392nd Ave
Aberdeen, SD 57401
Phone: (605) 229-0072

Notes: Located at intersection of 130th Street and 392nd Avenue

W. Brown Farm (FF-M)
45622 207th Street
Arlington, SD 57212
(605) 203 1003, (605) 983 3353, & (605) 983 4622 (fax)
Contact: Walter P. & Christine Brown
Notes: Located on north side of road, between 456th Ave. and 457th Ave. One of the oldest farms in the country, founded 1938. Double row sheds and outdoor row pens. 15 sheds.

Kingswood Mink Ranch (FF-M)
39231 281st Street
Armour, SD 57313
Phone: (605) 724-2696 or (605) 724-2660
Contact: Charles R. Larson
Notes: Large fur farm. Located east of US Highway 281. South side of the road.

Anderson Farm (FF-F)
Box 251
Brandt SD 57218
Contact: Rod Anderson
Notes: Unconfirmed. Street address needed.

Clinton Clark (FF-F)
RR3, Box #145
Clark, SD 57225
Phone: (605) 532-5209
Notes: Street address needed.

Mark Neilson (FF-F)
20795 441st Avenue
Lake Preston SD57249
Phone: (605) 983-5933
Notes: Located north of 205th Street.

Jo Meserve (FF-F)
13940 375th Avenue
Mina, SD 57451
Contact: Stephen R Meserve, Jo A Meserve

Utah

Total mink imprisoned (2019 USDA statistics): 876,000

Williams Fur Farm (FF-M)
11240 N 6000 W
American Fork, UT
Contact: Ann & Gordan Williams
Notes: 11 sheds. Dense residential neighborhood directly E of sheds. Backyards of subdivision homes connect with the farm fence.

Groves Mink Farm (FF-M)
5000 W 7300 South
Benjamin, UT 84660

Dixon Mink (FF-M)
15028 Pony Express Road
Bluffdale, UT 84065
Phone: (801) 495-0791
Contact: Loran D. Dixon
Notes: Farm is surrounded by a tall metal fence. Located directly south of office park.

Kenneth Dawson (FF-M)
430 N. Main St.
Coalville, UT 84017
Phone: (435) 336-5675

Don, Lori & Jason Winters (FF-M)
470 N. Main Street
Coalville, UT 84017
Phone: (435) 336-2326

BK Mink Ranch (FF-M)
551 South Main
Coalville UT 84017
Buster, Clarence & Edward Keyes
Phone: (435) 336 5904
Notes: Next to abandoned storefronts.
Located south of Old Farm Lane, east
side of road.

Rees Fur Farm (FF-M)
934 S. Hoytsville Road
Coalville UT 84017
Phone: (435) 336-3416
Contact: Dennis Rees, Ward Rees
Notes: Located on west side of road.
Dennis Rees is a former board member
of American Legend Cooperative. Large
farm. Approximately 54,000 mink.

Blonquist-Black Mink Farm (FF-M)
2 N 200 E
Coalville, UT
Phone: (435) 336-5595
Contact: Afton W. Blonquist, Gena &
Glen Black
Notes: Fence around sheds. Shallow
creek around south and east of property
on Park Rd. Borders county fairgrounds
on the west. Most visible from Park Rd.
Sheds directly adjoin shallow creek on
west side of fairgrounds parking lot.

Vernon Mink Farm (FF-M)
820 S. Hoytsville Road
Coalville, UT 84017
Phone: (435) 336-5982
Contact: Kent & NaVee Vernon
Notes: Located on west side of road.

Dean Vernon & Sons (FF-M)
391 E. Chalk Creek Road
Coalville, UT 84017
Phone: (435) 336-2376

Contact: Dean Vernon
Notes: Located on north side of road.
Chalk Creek Road is also known as
Highway 133. Five sheds. Still a large
farm.

fur farm (FF-M)
1246 S Hoytsville Rd (address approximate)
Coalville, UT
Notes: South of Adgel Lane. Two sheds
visible off road, west side.

Dixon Mink (FF-M)
15028 Pony Express Rd
Draper, UT
Notes: Between a storage complex and
office park. Farm is very close to I-15,
just south of Utah State Prison. Very tall
(10+ feet) metal wall surrounding sheds.
Trailer and house directly east of sheds.
Empty land to the west. All sheds were
completely enclosed and walled-in.

Jonsson, McLachlan fur farms (FF-M)
North 16000 West
Eagle Mountain, UT 84043
Notes: Two adjoining properties

Wardell Fur Farm (FF-M)
2425 W. Old Highway Road
Enterprise, UT 84050
Contact: Gail Wardell, Jay Wardell, Wess
Wardell
Phone: (801) 876-3418 or (801) 876-
3216 or (801) 876-3344
Notes: Large farm. Enterprise is north of
Morgan. Visible from I-84. 30 Sheds.

Gilbert McLachlan (FF-M)
14321 S Goshen Bay Road
Goshen, UT 84633
Phone: (801) 667-9935

J & G Mink Ranch; Highland, Utah

Dixon Mink; Draper Utah

Jenson Fur Farm; Logan, Utah

Ovard Mink Farm; Wanship, Utah

Stephens Fur Farms (FF-M)
Dallan J. Stephens
2475 E Canyon Rd
Henefer, UT 84033
Notes: Address is unconfirmed. This farm previously listed in The Final Nail print version with a PO Box address only. May be two sheds off East Canyon Rd, 3.4 miles (driving distance) from I-84. Southwest side of a dead-end, unmarked road with no other structures. Uninvestigated.

J & G Mink Ranch (FF-M)
10320 North 6400 West
Highland, UT 84003
Phone: (801) 756-5477
Contact: Glen Degelbeck
Notes: Six sheds. Very residential neighborhood. Best viewed via dirt road / bike path on N side of property. Stream to the N of dirt road, parallel. House to the S of sheds. Large neighborhood park across street.

Erekson Mink Ranch (FF-M)
11240 N 6000 W
Highland, UT 84003
Phone: (801) 756-6276
Contact: Tim Meredith Erekson
Notes: Located north of Highland Highway/Highway 92. 11 sheds. Located north of Highland Highway/Highway 92. Street address is approximate.

Gilbert McLachlan (FF-M)
14321 S. Goshen Bay Road
Goshen, UT 84633
Phone: (801) 667-9935

Bullock Farm (FF-F)
6240 W. 4700 S.
Hooper UT 84315-9749
Contact: Carl Bullock

Notes: Uninvestigated. Address may be residence.

Mitchell Olsen (FF-M)
350 W 6800 S
Hyrum, UT 84319
Phone: (435) 245-4739 or (801) 245-4384

Blackridge Farms (FF-M)
181 E 6400 S
Hyrum, UT 84319
Phone: (435) 245-6467 or (435) 245-6143
Contact: Lynn & Tama Mathews
Notes: Located south of the city, east of Highway 165, north of E 6600 S. Farm is next to Rosehill Dairy. Corn field service road leading to rear of farm on south. Surrounded by solid metal wall.

Lodder's Mink Farm (FF-M)
Kaysville/Farmington, UT 84025
Contact: Chuck & Shelly Lodder
Notes: No house on site. Located west of intersection of Sharpshooter Drive and Fox Hunter Drive, south of the Central Davis Sewer District Wastewater Treatment Plant (2200 South Sunset Drive, Kaysville, UT 84037).

Dane L. Dixon Mink Ranch (FF-M)
10725 N 8200 W
Lehi, UT
Phone: (801) 768-8721
Notes: Many streets in Lehi have more than one name, and alternate address is: intersection of W 3200 N and N 300 W (SW corner). "Mink Operation" sign posted. House directly E of sheds. Solid metal wall fence surrounding sheds. Large field directly W of property. Adjacent to subdivision and church. Farm announced it was relocating to an unknown address in late-2019.

Jonsson & Sons Mink Ranch (FF-M)
9250 W 8170 N
Lehi, UT 84043
Notes: Tall wooden wall around property. Across street from park / parking lot.

K&S Furs (FF-M)
7814 N 8730 W
Lehi, UT 84043
Phone: (801) 768-8573
Contact: Kenny Jensen

Jonsson & Sons Mink Ranch / Cedar Valley Fur Farm (FF-M)
9250 W 8170 N
Lehi, UT 84043
Phone: (801) 768-8075
Contact: Keith & Laurel Jonsson
Notes: Located across from the Lehi City Sports Park. W 8170 N is also known as W 700 S.

fur farm (FF-M)
Intersection of W 8170 N (also known as W 700 S) and dirt road immediately W of S 2575 W
Lehi, UT
Notes: No house on site. Well hidden, at end of small, unmarked dirt road. Road is new and not reflected on maps. Very close to new residential neighborhood. Large. Accessible via hidden dirt road on N from residential neighborhood. 20 Long sheds.

K & J Fur Farm (FF-M)
1440 West Main / West 73
Lehi, UT 84043
Contact: Kim Beckstead
Notes: Moat on W side. Very busy street. West Main Street is also known as W 8570 N (approximate address of farm: 8918 W 8570 N).

Willes Fur Farm (FF-M)
7878 W 8170 N
Lehi, UT
Phone: (801) 768-0402
Contact: Mike & June Willes
Notes: Located at southwest corner of W 8170 N and S 300 E. Small farm. Four long sheds. Partially wooden/partially metal fence surrounding property. Wooden fence in front. Residential neighborhood. Very busy street. Four farms on 8170 N.

Dell Willes (FF-M)
600 S 400 W
Lehi, UT 84043
Contact: Dell A. Willes, J Lene Willes
Phone: (801) 768-9120 or (801) 768-8171
Notes: 12 sheds long. Trailer on site. Very busy street. Heavy fence on street side, absent on other sides. Across the street from a church.

.

River Jordan Mink Ranch (FF-M)
9330 N 10400 W
Lehi, UT 84043
Phone: (801) 766-1305 or (801) 768-4491
Contact: Scott Cooper McLachlan
Notes: At one time this may have been the largest fur farm in the country. 100,000 mink. Located at corner of N 10400 W and W 9600 N, just west of the Jordan River. 100+ sheds. House directly N of farm. Large empty gated lot on SW side. Close to shopping center on UT-73/Main St. Two clusters of sheds. Operational center / processing & storage buildings in southern cluster of sheds, house at north. Three complexes located at corner of N 10400 W and W 9600 N, just west of the Jordan River.

K & J Fur Farm (FF-M)
1440 West Main Street
Lehi, UT 84043
Phone: (801) 768-8544
Contact: Kim D. Beckstead
Notes: West Main Street is also known as W 8570 N (approximate address of farm: 8918 W 8570 N).

Beckstead Fur Farm (FF-M)
3450 W 1500 North
Lehi, UT 84043

Egbert Mink / Northern Prairie Farms (FF-M)
1725 W 2000 S
Lewiston, UT 84320
Phone: (435) 258-5264
Contact: Gary R. Egbert
Notes: Sheds located on east and west sides of S 1600 W, south of W 2000 S (located just north of large egg farm).

Fur Breeder's Agricultural Co-op - Logan plant (FFFS)
1000 W 200 N
Logan, UT
Phone: (435) 752-5441
Contact: Chad Womack, Manager
Notes: Major feed production plant. Delivers to all FBAC clients north of Morgan, as far north as Grace, ID. On SE corner of intersection, across from Texaco. Second plant in Sandy.

Bohm Mink Farm (FF-M)
3490 W 600 S
Logan, UT 84321
Contact: Lance W. Bohm
Notes: Four sheds visible behind house number 3819 on N side of road. Nothing seen at 3490 W 600 S. Sheds directly behind house. Streams on both sides of house/sheds.

Jenson Fur Farm (FF-M)
715 S 1000 W
Logan, UT 84321
Phone: (435) 752-0184
Contact: Cordell O. Jenson
Notes: Many cows on property.

fur farm (FF-M)
S 3800 W
Logan, UT 84321
Notes: Located north of Mendon Road, west of S 3600 W.

Jenson Fur Farm (FF-M)
715 S 1000 W
Logan, UT 84321
Phone: (435) 752-0184
Contact: Cordell O. Jenson, Bruce Jenson
Notes: Located south of Mendon Road.

L & S Fur Farm (FF-M)
220 N Morgan Valley Drive
Morgan, UT 84050
Phone: (801) 829-3748
Contact: Larry Peterson
Notes: Large farm. Street address is approximate. Sheds very close road. Corporate address: 75 N Morgan Valley Drive.

Tony Jones Fur Farm (FF-M)
1016 South Highway 66
Morgan, UT 84050
Phone: (801) 829-6351
Contact: Tony & Tresa Jones
Notes: At end of dirt road. Dirt road very east to miss / address unmarked. South of Landmark Lane,

Dawson Mink Farm (FF-M)
50 Kippen West 2750 Lane S (alt. 50 W 2750 S)

Morgan, UT 84050
Phone: (801) 829-0623
Contact: Darin Dawson
Notes: Located south of the city, off of Highway 66/East Canyon Road.

fur farm (FF-M)
2850 S Morgan Valley Rd (approximate address)
Morgan, UT
Notes: Unconfirmed, yet sheds visible.

fur farm (FF-M)
810 or 820 E 100 S
Morgan, UT
Notes: South side of road. Directly W of dirt road for Wilkinson Construction. Large field W of sheds. House N of sheds.

Sargent Mink Ranch (FF-M)
707 E 100 S
Morgan, UT
Notes: North side of road. Barbed wire fence surrounding property. Large farm.

S. Francis Fur Farm (FF-M)
707 W Young Street
Morgan, UT 84050
Contact: Scott L. Francis, Jeff S. Francis
Notes: Located south side of road, west of Valarie Street.

Boyce Brothers Fur Farm (FF-M)
860 E 525 N
Morgan, UT 84050
Phone: (801) 829-6024
Bryan P. Boyce, Charles P. Boyce
Notes: 15 sheds. S side of 525 road. Barely visible from road.

Potter Mink (FF-M)
773 N 700 E
Morgan, UT 84050

Contact: JoAnn Potter
Notes: Located south side of road, next to Morgan City Cemetery. Single shed at rear of property. Status unconfirmed.

Round Valley Mink Ranch / Softmink (FF-M)
2000 E. Rees Lane
Morgan, UT 84050
Phone: (801) 829-3358
Contact: Stan & Kendra Rees
Notes: Directly off the exit, visible from Interstate 84. Sign reads "Rees Bros Hereforts". Large farm.

Dillree Fur Farm (FF-M)
1835 W. Stoddard Lane
Morgan, UT 84050
Phone: (801) 829-6368
Contact: Smokey & Barbara Dillree
Notes: South side of road. Mailbox adorned with a wooden mink sculpture. Two other clusters of sheds nearby, one of which may be part of Dillree farm. Possibly three farms on this road.

fur farm (FF-M)
Property next to 1835 W. Stoddard Lane
Morgan, UT 84050
Notes: Property west of Dillree Fur Farm.

Largent Fur Farm (FF-M)
2001 W Stoddard Lane
Morgan, UT 84050
Contact: Theodore Largent
Notes: Southwest of Dillree Fur Farm.

Thurston Fur Farm / Circle Bar Investments (FF-M)
1340 Island Road
Morgan, UT 84050
Phone: (801) 829-3858 or (801) 829-6327

Wardell Fur Farm; Enterprise, Utah

Margetts Mink Ranch; West Jordan, Utah

Round Valley Mink Ranch, Morgan, Utah

Dawson Mink Farm; Morgan, Utah

Spotlight
Fur Breeder's Agricultural Co-op

FBAC is the largest cooperatively owned feed supplier in the country. It has two locations: Sandy, Utah, and Logan, Utah.

Fur Breeders Agricultural Co-op (FBAC) - Sandy plant
8700 S 700 W
Sandy, UT 84070
Chris Falco: General Manager
Cody Mathews: President
Dale Christensen: Secretary
Susan: answers phones at main office.
Phone: (801) 255-4228 & (801) 289-4228
Head of research: Austin E. Larsen
Notes: Location #1 of this mink research farm and major feed production plant. Experimental feed research farm also on the property, at SW of property. Delivers to all member farms as far north as Morgan. On Jordan River.

The co-op has several delivery routes. The following is one feed delivery route which left the co-op @ 2am, as of 2009. Many of these farms have since closed.

1. Departs the Sandy plant. (2:10am)
2. Wardell Fur Farm, Morgan.
3. Boyce Brothers, Morgan.
4. Seth Dawson, Morgan (4am).
5. (Visits one to three other farms in Morgan after the Seth Dawson farm, before Round Valley).
6. Round Valley Mink Ranch, Morgan (5am).
7. Black Willow Mink, Coalville (5:40am).
8. (May visit one or two farms after Black Willow, before BK Mink Ranch)
9. BK Mink Ranch, Coalville (6:20am)
10. (Driver often takes nap in truck outside Polar King restaurant on Main Street, then has breakfast inside @ 7am)
11. Leaves Polar King, Coalville (8am).

12.   Rees' Fur Farm, Coalville (8:05am).
13.   Ovards, Wanship (8:30am).
14.   D&B Fur Farm, Peoa (9am).
15.   G-W Fur Farm, Peoa (9:15am).
16.   Return to Sandy plant.

Fur Breeder's Agricultural Co-op (Logan plant)
1000 W 200 N
Logan, UT
Phone: (435) 752-5441
Contact: Chad Womack, Manager
Notes: Major feed production plant. Delivers to all FBAC clients north of Morgan, as far north as Grace, ID. On SE corner of intersection, across from Texaco. Second plant in Sandy.

Fur Breeder's Agricultural Co-op; Logan, Utah

Fur Breeder's Agricultural Co-op; Logan, Utah

FBAC driver delivering mink feed to Utah fur farm

Fur Breeder's Agricultural Co-op; Sandy, Utah

Contact: Fred N. & Jean Thurston
Notes: At end of Island Rd.

Stan Stuart Fur Farm (FF-M)
750 E 100 S
Morgan, UT 84050
Phone: (801) 829-3347
Contact: Stan A. Stuart
Notes: South side of street. Located next
to Morgan Valley Polaris/Wilkinson
Construction.

Waldron Fur Farm (FF-M)
1125 S Morgan Valley Drive
Morgan, UT 84050

American Mink Council (FFO)
PO Box 548
Morgan, UT 84050
Phone: (801) 845-5174
Contact: Bryan Boyce, President
Notes: Marketing cooperative of mink
farmers.
Board of Directors:
Brad Wiebensohn: NAFA committee
Kyle Patrick: Vice President/Quality
Control
Scott Gamroth: President/ Chairman QC
Charles Mueller: Quality Control
Allen Moyle: Quality Control
Chuck Lodder: Region 3
David Schmitt, Jr.: Secretary/Treasurer
Dan Posch: Region 5
Gerald Trimberger: Director at Large
Jim Zimbal: Director At Large

fur farm (FF-M)
UT-116 [State Route 116]
Moroni, UT 84646
Notes: East of town, south of Blue Hill
Rd. West side of road.

fur farm (FF-M)
Franson Lane
"South Summit" (county?), UT
(Possibly Oakley, UT)
Notes: Farmer reported suspicious
vehicle at mink farm on Franson Lane
in "South Summit", UT, late-2009. The
only known "Franson Lane" is in Oakley, UT 84055.

Red Rock Farms (Choice Farms) (FF-M)
7528 S 5600 W
Payson, UT 84651
Phone: (801) 756-0106 or (801) 756-
2047
Contact: Dixie & Chad Fenn
Notes: Farm entrance may be located off
of W 7300 S.

G.W. Fur Farm (FF-M)
4811 N. Woodenshoe Lane
Peoa, UT 84061
Phone: (435) 783-5295
Contact: Wendell J. & Ila Stembridge
Notes: Located just south of the Peoa
Rodeo Grounds. 23 sheds.

Mont B Williams (FF-M)
5515 N. State Road 32
Peoa, UT 84061
Phone: (435) 783-5296

Rocky Top Fur Farm (FF-M)
5626 N State Road 32
Peoa, UT 84061
Contact: Gregory & Susan White
Notes: Located on hill above road.
Across the street from Marchant's Fur
Farm.

Marchant's Fur Farm (FF-M)
5739 N. State Road 32
Peoa, UT 84061
Phone: (435) 783-5671

Contact: Norval S. Marchant
Notes: Located on west side of road.

fur farm (FF-M)
592 N Main Street
Providence, UT 84332
Notes: Located east side of road, between E 550 N and E 650 N. Newly constructed residential neighborhood E of sheds. Barbed wire fence surrounding sheds/property. Neighborhood cul-de-sac points right at eastern-most shed @ 500 N and 140 E.

JM Bell, Inc. (FF-M)
345 S. Main Street
Randolph, UT 84064
Contact: John & Joann Bell
Notes: Located at SW corner of S. Main and Duck Street. Farm may be closed (investigation needed).

LS Carson Mink Ranch (FF-M)
1553 N 950 East
Richfield, UT 84701
Phone: (801) 735-7161
Contact: Larry S. Carson

Fur Breeders Agriculture Cooperative (FFFS)
8700 S 7th Street W.
Sandy, UT 84070
Contact: Christopher Falco, CEO/General Manager
Cody Mathews: President
Dale Christensen: Secretary
Susan: answers phones at main office.
Phone: (801) 255-4228 & (801) 289-4228
Notes: Fur farm feed supplier and mink farm. "Fur Breeders operates two production plants located in Sandy and Logan, Utah; these plants mix raw ingredients to make feed." At same address: Utah Fur Breeders Association. 7th

Street is also known as S 700 W. Located on west side of street, on the Jordan River. Mink sheds at SW of property. Experimental feed research farm also on the property. Fur industry sources state mink no longer kept on site, however this is unconfirmed. Houses and trailers in front/E of sheds. Large feed production building. Delivers to all member farms as far north as Morgan. The complex was heavily damaged in a December 2011 fire; the plant may not be in operation.

McMullin Farm (FF-M)
1350 W 5000 N
Smithfield, UT 84335
Phone: (435) 563-9336
Contact: Don & Corey McMullin
Notes: Located between N 1600 W and N 1200 W, south side of road. Narrow stretch of trees and thick brush line property to the N. House is at a great distance from the sheds.

McMullin & Sons Fur Farm (FF-M)
10471 S 1540 W
South Jordan, UT 84095
Phone: (801) 254-2817
Lindsey McMullin and son Brett
Notes: Small farm with 4,000 mink. 8 sheds. Dense residential neighborhood. Close to strip malls & a busy road.

LS Carson Mink Ranch (location #2) (FF-M)
6199 South 2800 West
Spanish Fork, Utah 84660

Shoreline Feeds (FFFS)
6245 So 2800 West
Spanish Fork, Utah 84660
Phone: 801-756-0106

MinkMod (FFES)
1196 South Mill Road
Spanish Fork, UT 84660
Phone: (801) 369-7692
Contact: Daniel Davis
Notes: Manufacturer of "carcass tumbler" and other processing equipment for mink farmers.

Blue Star Ranch (FF-M)
2329 W 7300 S
Spanish Fork, UT 84660
Phone: (801) 798-9631
Contact: David Davis

Westwood Mink (FF-M)
8137 S 1800 W
Spanish Fork, UT 84660
Phone: (801) 798-1786
Contact: Paul Westwood
Notes: Sheds close to house. Located south of W 8000 S/Highway 164.

Van Dyke Mink Farm (FF-M)
2700 Canyon Road
Springville, UT 84663
Contact: Robert Van Dyke
Notes: 5 sheds. Small farm. Located south side of road. Shallow stream behind sheds. Large undeveloped residential neighborhood in rear of farm. Bike path runs along back, feet from sheds. Sheds at great distance from the house.

Ovard Mink Farm (FF-M)
1715 S. Hoytsville Road
Wanship, UT 84017
Phone: (435) 336-5820
Contact: Harold G. Ovard
Notes: Small farm. Approximately 1,200 mink. No fence. On dirt driveway E of Hoytsville Rd. Fields to N and S of

property. At least one shed empty.

Margetts Mink Ranch (FF-M)
1975 Canal Road (1975 W 6670 S)
West Jordan, UT 84084
Phone: (801) 969-7555
Contact: Cory & Christy Margetts
Notes: Located on south side of road. House in front/directly N of sheds. Chain link fence surrounding sheds. On dead end road.

fur farm (FF-M)
8860 S 5600 W
West Mountain, UT 84651
Notes: Street address is approximate. Farm located on west side of S 5600 W, just south of W 8800 S.

Kenneth Vernon Mink Ranch (FF-M)
285 E. Center Street
Wooodruff, UT 84086
Phone: (435) 793-4246
Contact: Kenneth L. Vernon
Notes: Single shed visible. Status inconclusive.

Virginia

Steve Colvin (FF-F)
2000 SB Road
Barboursville, VA 22923
Notes: Unconfirmed. Associated with the live penning of foxes & possible fur farm.

Jerry Pangle (FF-F)
21693 Dovesville Road
Bergton, VA 22811-2210
Notes: Unconfirmed. Associated with the live penning of foxes. Possible fur farm.

Washington

Total mink imprisoned (2019 USDA statistics): 55,000

Northwest Farm Food Co-op (FFFS)
1370 S. Anacortes Street
Burlington, WA 98233
Phone: (360) 757-4225
Fax: (360) 757-8206
Contact: Jim Rowe, General Manager;
Harvey Beck, President

Jerry Marr (FF-M)
4799 Mount Baker Highway
Deming, Washington 98244
Phone: (360) 592-5051
Notes: 18 miles west of the Dale Marr
Black Plush ranch. Between Scarlett Way
& Mitchell Rd, south side of road.

Marr Mink Farm (FF-M)
9216 Cornell Creek Road
 -and-
9580 Mount Baker Highway
 -and-
9471 Cornell Creek Road
Deming, WA 98244
Phone: (360) 599-2881
Contact: Dale & Dawn Marr
Notes: Cornell Creek Road is just south
of Mt. Baker Highway. Second cluster of
sheds just north, on Mt. Baker Hwy.

Miller's Mink Ranch (FF-M)
2823 Addy Gifford Road
Gifford, WA 99131
Phone: (509) 722-6334
Mike & Gina Miller

United Farms (FF-M)
23212 86th Avenue E
Graham, WA 98338

Phone: (253) 847-2345
Contact: Dale Pederson
Notes: "Twelve species of fur bearing animals" (Fur Rancher Magazine). Wolves reported as among the species. Large farm. Not visible from road. Located west of 86th Ave. Near very residential neighborhoods. Several layers of fencing around property. Sheds at a distance from the house.

Beck's Mink Farm (FF-M)
17903 Engebretsen Road
Granite Falls, WA 98252
Phone: (360) 691-6308
Contact: Harvey & Gincy Beck
Notes: No house on site. At same address, Olympic Fur Breeders Association. Harvey Beck is President, Northwest Farm Food Co-op (as of 2012).

Washington State University (FR)
Department of Veterinary Microbiology & Pathology
1040 NE Airport Road
Pullman WA 99164
Phone: (509) 335-7321
Notes: WSU fur industry researcher John R. Gorham died in October 2011. Dr. Gorham received funding from the fur industry for many years, including a $10,000 grant from Fur Commission USA in 2010, to study diseases in mink. David J. Prieur, also at WSU, has also received funding from Fur Commission USA. The university has told the media it no longer does mink research, however this is unconfirmed. Investigation needed. Also employed by WSU is Jason Roesler, who is on the board of the Fur Com-

Spotlight
Washington State University

While its claims should be taken with extreme skepticism, the university has publicly stated it no longer performs mink research on campus. What is confirmed is that leading fur industry & WSUs researcher John Gorham has retired. Yet his protégé, David J. Prieur, remains at WSU and has also received grants from the Fur Commission USA.

While the status of Washington State University's mink research is in question, we present this report as both offering relevant clues as to where mink research may be occurring, as well as insight into (non-fur-industry-related) wildlife research at WSU.

Received anonymously

Washington State University mink research facility: An investigation

Washington State University
Wildlife Bio Animal Holding Facility
3055 Antelope Trail
Pullman, WA

Submitted anonymously.

"When the call went out soliciting the location of the USDA Fur Bearer Research Facility in Pullman, WA; we made the drive to locate the research farm ourselves. It's been speculated the better part of the fur farm addresses we have today were confiscated from fur industry research labs raided during Operation Bite Back. One address that never surfaced was for one of the facilities raided, the USDA Fur Bearer Research Facility at Washington State University...

The A.L.F.-authored publication Memories of Freedom – an anonymous account of every (claimed) action in Operation Bite Back – offers the only published information giving clues on the research farm's whereabouts. Extracted from Chapter Four, we had only these crumbs of info to aid in our search:

- The farm was surrounded by barbed wire
- On the "outskirts" of campus
- Surrounded by grassland
- "…on a road to the local airport."

With little information to work with, we made the long drive to Pullman, WA to find the farm.

We quickly narrowed the area that could potentially house the research farm to the various ag-research animal pens along Airport Road, on WSU's eastern edge. As described in M.O.F., along Airport Road we found pens of grizzly bears, sheep, goats, cows, and numerous other exotic and non-exotic species confined to small pens by WSU's expansive animal research machine.

At night, we explored the small labyrinth of dirt roads and paths along Airport Road on foot. In four hours, after inspecting numerous sheds, pens, and barns, we had narrowed potential sites for the farm to two locations:

1. Two sheds of empty cages behind 1040 NE Airport Road.
2. A fenced outdoor facility off a dirt road adjacent to Wilson Rd, housing various sheds and pens.

Evidence pointing to the former was its location close to the only known address associated with WSU mink research: "1040 NE Airport Rd". The sheds approximated the design of mink sheds, if bisected lengthwise. However the feeding devices on the cages appeared to more closely resemble those for birds than mink. And there was no grassy hill above the sheds, as described in M.O.F. Nothing else found near this address was likely to house mink. We took numerous photos of the two sheds for future review.

Our strongest suspicions fell on a heavily secured facility tucked a quarter mile from Airport Road.

Binoculars failed to reveal what was inside, but certain large animal pens were visible, along with a large shed and barn. We left to do more research and return the following night for a closer look – and final answer.

The next morning we reviewed old campus maps in the library, and older archived satellite images. One thing stood out: images from the early-1990s show two long sheds in an area inspected the night before, where there was now a vacant field. Their long and narrow form would make it unlikely they housed anything other than mink. Comparing new and old images revealed something further: While the sheds had been demolished, the fenced area under suspicion from the night before had been greatly expanded.

Had the WSU consolidated its wildlife research into one secured facility after the 1992 A.L.F. raid?

The next night we made the hike back to this location. The site is hidden off a dark, unmarked dirt road (later learned to be called "Antelope Trail") branching east off Airport Road. Unlike every other animal facility off Airport Rd, this one was heavily secure, with a high barbed-wire fence, motion sensor spotlights, several video cameras, and heavy lighting. At the rear of the facility, we found numerous animal pens. When our eyes adjusted to the darkness, we found ourselves face to face with numerous deer, confined to small pens.

We spent many minutes sharing the silence of the night with these animals, staring at us from behind two layers of fencing.

Beyond the deer pens, a large shed in the center had its contents mostly obscured, and any animals that may be inside were not visible.

On the north, elevated just above the compound and outside its fence, were three outdoor animal pens that were found empty.

Inside the pens were red lights indicating alarms (or merely the appearance of them to serve as a deterrent). We moved towards the most suspicious portion of the site: the low-lying sheds in the NE corner, where we suspected the mink were housed. The obscured siding told us whatever was inside was not domesticated enough to live in a totally enclosed structure, but was something the animals' captors wanted shielded from public view. We were within 20 feet of the pens when, from inside, a red flashlight began moving towards us.

We vanished into the grasslands, just short of an answer as to what lay inside the sheds at 3055 Antelope Trail.

The following day we returned in daylight for photos, which are being submitted with this report.

Although inconclusive, evidence indicates that 3055 Antelope Trail is the most likely location for the mink imprisoned at W.S.U. A review of the evidence:

- Its level of security is commensurate with a facility fearing a(nother) break-in, and inconsistent with security at all other animal pens at WSU (where security is absent).
- A WSU building list puts the address as a "Wildlife Bio Animal Holding Facility"
- Allowing for the possibility this facility housed mink at the time of the A.L.F. raid; there are several animal pens (large enough for coyotes) on a hill just above this facility, consistent with the M.O.F. description (coyotes were released during the A.L.F. action from a "hill above the fur farm").
- WSU describes this address as housing deer "...and other wildlife species".
- The low-lying sheds in back are consistent with the general height of mink sheds, a height unique to structures housing mink (among commonly raised livestock).
- Barring the possibility the research farm has been moved to an entirely different part of campus since the A.L.F. raid, our extensive survey of the "road to the local airport" found these to be the only pens whose captives we could not confirm, and the only location
- Found with the potential to house mink.

The combined evidence and photos make a strong but inconclusive case for 3055 Antelope Trail as being the location of the experimental fur farm.

Anonymous"

Washington State University
"Wildlife Bio Animal Holding Facility"

mission USA's committee for animal welfare and government affairs and related to the Roesler mink farming family in Sultan, WA.

Brick Road Fur Farm (FF-M)
19780 NE 55th Place (alt. 5616 196th Avenue NE)
Redmond, WA 98053
Phone: (425) 868-4192
Contact: Blair & Mary Hudson
Notes: Mary Hudson is Vice President, Olympic Fur Breeders Association (as of 2012).

Roesler Brothers Fur Farm (FF-M)
33425 138th Street SE
Sultan, WA 98294
Phone: (360) 793-0429
Contact: Brad & Kate Roesler, Jeff Roesler
Notes: Located on a dirt road west of 339th Avenue SE, north of the McDonalds on US Hwy. 2. West of 339th Avenue SE, north of US Hwy. 2. Brad Roesler is President, Olympic Fur Breeders Association (as of 2012) and Vice President, Northwest Farm Food Co-op (as of 2012). Kate Roesler is former Secretary of Fur Commission USA. Sheds surrounded by dense forest. Electronic perimeter security.

Olsen Mink Ranch (FF-M)
4695 Reese Hill Road
Sumas, WA 98295
Notes: Farm reported closed (investigation needed).

Schader Mink Ranch (FF-M)
19726 SE 128th Avenue

Yelm, WA 98597
Contact: Robert M. & Marjorie C. Schader
Notes: Unconfirmed. Address obtained from business records.

Wisconsin

Total mink imprisoned (2019 USDA statistics): 1.2 million

Wisco Feeds (FFFS)
114 S. First Street
Abbotsford, WI 54405
Phone: (715) 223-4211
Contact: Alwyn K. Pedersen
Notes: Building reads "Wisco Feeds". Office sign reads "Wayne Feeds; Wayne Animal Health Aids 223-4596" on front of office building.

Harold Widder (FF-F)
N 805 Christie Road
Antigo, WI 54409

Ewan Fur Farm (FF-M)
1846 County Road A
Athens, WI 54411
Phone: (715) 257-7333
Contact: Donald Ewan, Richard Ewan

Rothenberger Farm (FF-F)
1455 Windfall Hill Road
Athens WI 54411
Contact: Cheryl Rothenberger
Notes: Unconfirmed.

Joseph Schrock (FF-M)
S11481 Stinson Rd
Augusta WI 54722

Valenti Farm (FF-F)
PO Box 549
Baileys Habor WI 54202-0549
Contact: Don Valenti
Notes: Street address unknown.

Breezy Point Mink Ranch (FF-M)
W14152 Garden Valley Lane
Blair, WI 54616
Phone: (608) 989-2995
Contact: Judy Peters

Kovars Farm (FF-F)
2873 County Road M
Boscobel WI 53805
Contact: Dan Kovars
Notes: Unconfirmed.

Mark Ziemer (FF-F)
W14712 Old D Road
Bowler, WI 54416

Krieger Fur Farm (FF-M)
17320 93rd Street
Bristol, WI 53104
Phone: (262) 857-2079 or (262) 857-4060
Contact: Gerald R. Krieger
Notes: 93rd Street is also known as County Road C. 10+ foot wall of cages constructed around portions of farm.

Bill & Sandy Peterson (FF-F) 6682
Hospital Road Burlington, WI 53105
Phone: (262) 763-5623

Sherfield Farm (FF-M)
2947 N County Road FF
Butternut, WI 54514
Phone: (715) 476-2808
Contact: Dale & Cathy Sherfield

Notes: Located at corner of County Road FF and Miller Road, west side of road. Farm is located behind a bar called "Camp 1." Small mink farm. Breeding stock consists of 500 female and 125 male mink. Property was for sale as of November 2013.

Fur Harvesters Auction (FP)
400 England Street
Cambridge, WI 53523
Phone: (608) 423-4814 or (608) 225-9153
Contact: Greg Schroeder
Notes: Fur receiving and grading facility. Fur Harvesters Auction's corporate headquarters is located in Ontario, Canada. Major choke-point for the trapping industry.

Pagel Mink Ranch (FF-M)
W1095 County Road B
Campbellsport, WI 53010
Phone: (920) 477-4794 or (920) 477-4792
Contact: John & Carole Pagel, Joe Pagel
Notes: On north side of road. Sign reads, "Pagel's Mink Ranch - Established 1955 by Victor and Elaine Pagel." Possibly abandoned farm across the street, not visible from the road.

Wiesman Mink Ranch (FF-M)
W13311 Buss Road
Caroline, WI 54928
Phone: (715) 754-5645
Contact: Emil (Bud) & Karen Wiesman
Notes: Large fur farm. South side of road. Buss Road dead-ends at the farm. Sheds behind tall fence, directly on the road. Dogs present, but fenced off from

sheds. Also a hunting preserve which houses deer (Southbranch Preserve). Numerous signs posted reading "Deer Farm."

Burg Bros. Mink Ranch (FF-M)
W5450 Ecker Lakeland
Chilton, WI 53014
Phone: (920) 439-1737
Contact: Bennett & June Burg
Notes: Farm may be closed (investigation needed).

Den-Patt Fur Farms (FF)
Rural Route 3
Chippewa Falls, WI
Notes: Address unknown.

Dillenberg Farm (FF-M) (FF-F)
N2544 Hickory Lane
Clintonville, WI 54929
Phone: (715) 853-7002 or (715) 823-3694
Contact: Leo & Karen Dillenberg

Schultz Farm (FF-F)
N13053 Meridian
Colby WI 54421
Contact: Wayne Schultz

David Mink Ranch (FF-M)
N2172 South 27th Road
Coleman, WI 54112
Contact: Judith J. David
Notes: Farm may be closed (investigation needed).

LeFever Farm (FF-F)
Box 238
Coloma WI 54930
Contact: Mike LeFever
Notes: Street address unknown.

Shattuck Farm (FF-F)
N15627 Ronadka Avenue
Curtiss, WI 54422
Contact: Lynn Shattuck
Notes: Unconfirmed.

Brecke Farms (FF-M)
5986 Reynolds Avenue
Dorchester, WI 54425
Phone: (715) 654-5678
Contact: Gerald & Pat Brecke
Notes: Located at end of Reynolds Ave., just south of County Line Road. Sheds best visible from County Line Rd (Reynolds Ave is a dead end/driveway to farm). House N of sheds, in close proximity.

Jon Hackel (FF-M)
W983 Huckleberry Street
Edgar, WI 54426
Phone: (715) 352-3267
Notes: Located at intersection with Short Road.

Klubertanz Equipment Company (FFES)
1165 State Road 73
Edgerton, WI 53534
Phone: (800) 237-3899 or (608) 884-9481
Contact: Richard Klubertanz, President
Notes: Supplier of wire, cages and equipment to mink and fox farmers. Supplies "wire, hoppers, water cups, and / or other suppliers".

American Fur Farmers Association (FFO)
W8209 County Road H

Elkart Lake, WI
Notes: Fur farming organization ("second largest private treaty fur brokerage house in the world"). Current status unknown. Address is a house at the end of a long driveway.

T & T Mink (FF-M)
W1300 Sheboygan Road
Elkhart Lake, WI 53020
Phone: (920) 894-7688
Contact: Thomas Winkel
Notes: Street address is approximate. Located at southeast corner of Sexton Road and Sheboygan Road. Dilapidated barn on site. Barn may be a house, but it is likely there is no house on site. Directly east of Dean Foods Dairy.

Helbing Farm (FF-F)
N2007 Snyder Rd.
Elroy WI 53929-9710
Contact: Mike Helbing
Notes: Unconfirmed.

Evergreen Mink Ranch (FF-M)
W4970 Harmon Road
Elton, WI 54430
Phone: (715) 882-1100
Contact: Dale Christensen

Larson Mink Ranch (FF-M)
W4471 Buckner Road
Elton, WI 54430
Phone: (715) 882-2741
Contact: Dave Larson

Roger Woodford (FF-M)
S 101 S 150th Avenue
Fall Creek, WI 54742
Phone: (715) 877-3308

Muthig Industries (FFES)
33 East Larsen Drive
Fond du Lac, WI 54937
Phone: (920) 922-9814
Contact: Bruce W. Muthig, President
Notes: Manufacturer of pellet feeders for mink farms.

Cisewski Farm (FF-F)
S3208 Jumbeck Lane
Fountain City WI 54629
Contact: Bob Cisewski
Notes: Unconfirmed.

Kurhajec Fur Farm (FF-M)
9602 West 3 Mile Road
Franksville, WI 53126
Phone: (262) 835-2866 or (262) 835-4066
Contact: Jim & Shelly Kurhajec
Notes: Farm not visible from street; entrance just west of 96th Street.

Huebner Farm (FF-M)
N1405 Guhl Road
Fremont WI 54940
Contact: Merlyn Huebner
Notes: Unconfirmed.

Mink Veterinary Consulting and Research Service (FFO)
W8366 Spring Valley Dr,
Glenbeulah, WI 53023
Notes: 501c3 non profit as of 2013, "assisting with the coordination of critical vaccine supply." $7 million in revenue, 2013. Organization exists to buy vaccines in bulk at a discount from United Vaccines and distributes to fur farmers. Board members: John Easley, Gerald

Wall of cages, Krieger Fur Farm; Bristol, Wisconsin

Razor wire, Zimbal Minkery; Oostburg, Wisconsin

Gamroth Mink Ranch; Independence, Wisconsin

T & T Mink; Elkhart Lake, Wisconsin.

Trimberger, Brad Joyner, Scott Harris, Thomas Mclellan. Address may be John Easley's home address.

A&M Dittrich Mink Farm (FF-M)
N3984 Martin Dr
Goodrich, WI 54451
Notes: Newly constructed location of the A&M Dittrich Mink Farm.

LaBudde Group, Inc. (FFFS)
1239 12th Avenue
Grafton, WI 53024
Phone: (262) 375-9111
Contact: Richard T. Erickson

Gamroth Mink Ranch (FF-M)
W22577 State Road 121
Independence, WI 54747
Phone: (715) 985-3530 or (715) 985-3462
Contact: Scott & Allan Gamroth
Notes: Located next door to Smieja Fur Farm. State Road 121 is also known as Whitehall Road. On busy road. House at a distance from many of the sheds.

Twin Pine Fur Farm (Smieja Fur Farm) (FF-M)
W22875 State Road 121
Independence, WI 54747
Phone: (715) 985-3020 or (715) 985-3713
Contact: Tom & Jan Olson

Chelf's Mink Ranch (FF-M)
N7498 County Road H
Irma, WI 54442
Phone: (715) 453-8847
Contact: Michael J. & Diane Chelf
Notes: Located just south of Leach Road. County Road H is also known as County Road V. House at distance from sheds.

Autumn River Farms (FF-M)

W5379 Eagle Road
Juneau, WI 53039
Phone: (920) 204-8346
Contact: Mike & Marion Mclay, David McLay, Ryan Thoma
Notes: Located 1/2 mile west of State Hwy. 115, south side of road.

Sally Costabile (FF-M)
8941 Cooper Rd.
Kenosha, WI 53142
Notes: Unconfirmed. Appearance of a small farm on satellite images, just south of this address, south of corner @ 91st Place.

Langer Farms (FF-M)
N921 Norman Road / E3285 Fur Lane
Kewaunee, WI 54216
Phone: (920) 776-1207
Contact: James W. Langer, Kenneth J. Langer
Notes: Located just north of Sandy Bay Road. "Fur Lane" is the name given to the farm's driveway. Houses 20,000 mink as of 1997.

Hidden Acres Fur Farm (FF-F)
17930 Church Road
Kiel, WI 53042
Phone: (920) 773-2524
Contact: Phillip Endries, Pete Endries
Notes: Farm may be closed; may only operate as a rendering business (investigation needed). Located southwest of the village of St. Nazianz.

Borchardt Farm (FF-F)
7278 3rd Lane
Marathon WI 54448
Contact: Lanny Borchardt
Notes: Unconfirmed.

West Bay Fur (FF-M)
N2795 Shore Drive
Marinette, WI 54143
Phone: (715) 735-3732 or (715) 732-4894
Contact: Charles & Sharon LaCourt
Notes: Located north of Rader Road. Entrance to farm is just south of the Shore Crest bar.

Hecke Farm (FF-F)
12065 Lincoln Spencer Road
Marshfield WI 54449
Contact: David Hecke
Notes: Unconfirmed.

Medford Fur Food (FFFS)
N3528 State Highway 13
Medford, WI 54451
Phone: (715) 748-2255
Contact: Tony Kleifgen, Manager
Notes: Semi trucks and other vehicles visible on the property. On east side of Hwy 13.

Central Mink Foods (FFFS)
651 S. Whelan Avenue
Medford, WI 54451
Phone: (715) 748-3188
Contact: Bruce Jentzsch
Notes: On west side of road. Single building. One small delivery truck in rear with "Central Mink Foods" logo.

Romie Deml Mink Ranch (FF-M)
N3641County Road E
Medford, WI 54451
Contact: Romie Deml
Notes: Located south of Center Avenue; next to Kalmon's Fur Farm. No farm behind 3641 address. Farm is on the

SE corner of the CR-E and Center Ave intersection, across the street from this address.

Ed Dittrich Mink Ranch (FF-M)
879 E Perkins Street
Medford, WI 54451
Phone: (715) 748-4359
Contact: Edward Dittrich
Notes: Located near downtown Medford. One of the oldest farms in the country, founded 1928.

Mildbrand Mink Ranch (FF-M)
W5339 Whittlesey Avenue
Medford, WI 54451
Contact: Scott & Gail Mildbrand
Notes: Located just west of Highway 13. S side of road. House is barely visible from, but close to, road. Two dirt driveways on property. Sheds are S of house and barn, not visible from road. Imprisons 10,000 mink.

Jentzsch Mink Ranch (FF-M)
1195 S. 8th Street / Highway 13
Medford, WI 54451
Phone: (715) 748-4587
Contact: Bruce Albert Jentzsch
Notes: Large farm. Located just south of downtown Medford. Located just east of Central Mink Foods and south of Ed Dittrich Mink Ranch.

fur farm (FF-M)
W7521 Center Ave
Medford, WI 54451

Blasel Fur Farm (FF-M)
W3923 Apple Avenue
Medford, WI 54451

Halbach Mink Ranch; New Holstein, Wisconsin

National Feeds; New Holstein, Wisconsin

Pagel Mink Ranch; Campbellsport, Wisconsin

Wiesman Mink Ranch; Caroline, Wisconsin

Geiger Mink Farm; Mosinee, Wisconsin

Gessler's Mink Ranch; Tomahawk, Wisconsin

Golden Sands Ranch; Wild Rose, Wisconsin

Mildbrand Mink Ranch; Medford, Wisconsin

Phone: (715) 678-2501
Contact: Dennis & Amy Blasel

Kalmon's Fur Farm (FF-M)
N3647 County Road E
Medford, WI 54451
Phone: (715) 748-5506
Contact: George & Rita Kalmon
Notes: Located north of Center Avenue; next to Romie Deml Mink Ranch. Visible from Center Ave and CR-E. Long sheds W of house, in close proximity to farmer and neighbor's houses. "Kalmon" on mailbox.

A&M Dittrich Mink Farm (FF-M)
N3472 Grahl Drive
Medford, WI 54451
Phone: (715) 785-8000 or (715) 748-9839
Contact: Jorn Mogensen, Manager
Notes: Very large farm. Located just south of Center Avenue. Visible from Grahl Dr. and Center Ave. Watchtower NE of sheds.

Hugh Hildebrandt, DVM (FR)
Medford Veterinary Clinic
898 S. Gibson Street
Medford, WI 54451
Phone: (715) 748-2341
Notes: Fur industry researcher. Received numerous grants from the Fur Commission USA. Hildebrandt is editor of "Fur Animal Research Letter," a quarterly newsletter published by the Fur Commission USA.

Brian Kahnke (FF-M)
W10454 Stuhr Road
Melrose, WI 54642

Waschack Blue Haven Mink Ranch (FF-M)
W7015 Manitowoc Rd
Menasha, WI 54952
Phone: (920) 734-5201
Notes: Unconfirmed.

Neo-Dynamics
4738 Bergamot Way, Suite 200
Middleton, WI 53562
Phone: (800) 206-7227
Fax: (608) 831-4669
Contact: Tim J. Cairns
Notes: Manufacturer of melatonin implants (used by mink farmers to speed fur growth). Tim is also president of Melatek (www.melatek.net), a company that manufactures melatonin implants for ferrets and dogs. Melatek's "Principal Office", according to the Wisconsin Secretary of State, is 4738 Bergamot Way in Middleton, WI. Neo-Dynamics is registered in Colorado. According to the Colorado Secretary of State, the company's "Principal Street Address" is 625 N. Taft Hill Road, Fort Collins, CO 80521. Possible the drug is manufactured in Colorado, but marketed out of Wisconsin. This is the same company (or a new incarnation) of Wildlife Pharmaceuticals, a manufacturer of melatonin implants since the mid-1990s. Cairns is also a former (or current) fox farmer.

Sandy Bay Mink Ranch (FF-M)
2228 Cherney Road
Mishicot, WI 54228
Phone: (920) 755-2834 or (800) 999-2834
Contact: Brad L. Wiebensohn, Kurt

Wiebensohn

Notes: Large farm, with 30,000 animals (1997). Animals valued at 2.5 to 3 million dollars (1997). Farmer reports he raises mink "among other things" (1997). Located at corner of Cherney Road and W. Samz Road. Brad Wiebensohn is a Board Member, American Mink Council.

Dittrich Mink Ranch (Sanders Farm?) (FF-M)
N7446 County Road LS
Mosel, WI 53083
Contact: Gene D. Dittrich, Christel Sanders
Notes: Christel Sanders is President of the Kettle Moraine Mink Breeders Association.

Geiger Mink Farm (FF-M)
1000 Gardner Park Road
Mosinee, WI 54455
Phone: (715) 359-7839
Contact: Thomas & Barbara Geiger
Notes: Located at corner of Gardner Park Road and River Forest Lane; just east of the Wisconsin River. Gardner Park Rd is unmarked road just south of Weston Power Plant. Best view of farm is from footpath at end of Blueberry Lane (dead end road off Russell St), which leads directly to farm's rear. In a dense residential neighborhood.

fur farm (Oak Grove Fur Farm?) (FF-M)
W2359 County Road WH
Mount Calvary, WI 53057
Notes: Located at junction of County Road WH and County Road W, north side of road.

John A. Treutelaar (FF-F)
S79 W25925 National Avenue
Mukwonago, WI 53149
Phone: (262) 662-3714
Notes: Across street from Morningstar Golfers Club.

National Feeds (formerly National Fur Foods) (FFFS)
1310 Milwaukee Drive
New Holstein, WI 53061
Phone: (800) 558-5803 or (847) 715-6415
Contact: Dré Sanders, Director; Al Newman; salesperson.
Notes: At one time (possibly still) the largest fur farm feed supplier. Produces fox and mink feed. Owned by Milk Specialties Company (Dundee, IL). Large complex with feed mill building and separate building housing offices. On a very busy street. Dead-end residential road runs along the rear.

D & N Mink / Halbach Mink Ranch (FF-M)
W1314 Foundry Road
New Holstein, WI 53061
Phone: (920) 898-9195
Contact: Donald & Nancy Halbach, Scott Halbach
Notes: Located at corner of Foundry Road & Plymouth Trail.

Associated Fur Farms (FF-M)
N1326 County Road J
(Alternate address/same location: W846 Fur Farm Road)
New Holstein, WI 53061
Contact: R. Todd Langenfeld, Shaw C.

Kalmon's Fur Farm; Medford, Wisconsin

Medford Fur Foods; Medford, Wisconsin

Jentzsch Mink Ranch; Medford, Wisconsin

Central Mink Foods; Medford, Wisconsin

Langenfeld, Maxwell T. Langenfeld
Notes: Large farm. Located at corner of
County Road J and Fur Farm Road.

B & P Thelen Ranch (FF-M)
W830 Fur Farm Road
New Holstein, WI 53061
Phone: (920) 286-0929 or (920) 898-
5929
Contact: Brad & Paula Thelen
Notes: Located next to Associated Fur
Farms.

Bonlander Mink Ranch (FF-M)
W1597 Foundry Road
New Holstein, WI 53061
Phone: (920) 898-5607
Contact: Gary & Virginia Bonlander

Preissner Fur Farm (FF-M)
New Holstein, WI
Owner: Dennis Preissner, "Third generation fur farmer"
Notes: Information points to this farm
being open as of 2005. Address unknown. "Having to constantly watch my
property making sure someone is not
breaking in really takes its toll." (farmer
quote, 2005)

Magnuson Fur Farm (FF-M)
W2166 Forest Drive
Ogema, WI 54459
Phone: (715) 767-5480 or (715) 767-
5734
Contact: Herb Magnuson, Frank Mag-
nuson
Notes: Located at corner of Forest Drive
and Springdale Drive, off of County
Road C. House is on the opposite side
of the street.

Schuppel Mink Farm (FF-M)
436 S Court St
Onalaska, WI
Contact: Erwin Schuppel
Status: No farm at this address. Investi-
gation needed.

Smies Fur Farm (FF-M)
W1618 Smies Road
Oostburg, WI 53070
Contact: Abram Smies
Notes: Located on the west shore of
Lake Michigan. Sign posted announcing
a $500 reward from the Farm Bureau for
information leading to the conviction of
animal liberators. House close to sheds.

Zimbal Minkery (FF-M)
6020 Wilson Lima Road
Oostburg, WI 53070
Robert & Linda Zimbal
Phone: (920) 564-2118 or (920) 467-
8125
Notes: The two Zimbal farms are said
to form the largest mink farm in North
America. 40,000 breeding females
producing up to 5 kits a year (up to
240,000 mink imprisoned). Farm is
located at the end of Abraham Court,
off of County Trunk A. Railroad tracks
and convenient railroad service road run
along east side of farm. Robert Zimbal is
Treasurer, Fur Commission USA.

fur farm (FF-M)
9632 Sauk Trail Rd.
Oostburg, WI
Notes: W side of Sauk Trail Rd.

Voskull Mink Ranch (FF-M)
N2141 State Road 32
Oostburg, WI 53070
Contact: Martin Voskull
Notes: Located just north of Demaster Road. Farm may be closed (investigation needed).

George Valiga Sr. (FF-M)
Pine Lane
Phillips, WI 54555
Notes: Off Highway 13.

Frenchman's Folly Fox Farm (FF-F)
N10410 Pickerel Lake Road
Pickerel, WI 54465
Phone: (715) 484-5721
Contact: Lloyd & Nancy Bussiere

Blanke's Hilltop Fur Farm (FF-M)
W6343 State Road 67
Plymouth, WI 53073
Contact: Melvin O. Blanke
Phone: (920) 254-1526 or (920) 892-4287
Notes: Located east of Oak Road, southwest of the town of Plymouth. Mel Blanke is president of United Feeds, up the road.

United Feeds, Inc. (FFFS)
W8414 State Road 67
Plymouth, WI 53073
Phone: (920) 526-3211
Contact: Jim Wachter, Ryan Wachter, Melvin O. Blanke, President
Notes: Located west of the town of Plymouth. Large complex. Three buildings. Several semi trucks with "United Feeds" logo. Collectively owned among approximately 26 fur farmers.

John S. Easley, DVM (FR)
Dairy Doctors Veterinary Services
1020 S. Pleasant View Road
Plymouth WI 53073
Phone: 920-892-4696
Note: Leading fur industry consultant and vet, and expert in mink disease. Among his role in multiple fur industry organizations, he is head of the fur industry non-profit Mink Veterinary Consulting and Research. Through this organization, each year mink farmers purchase millions of dollars of vaccines from United Vaccines. Easley is also Director of Research, Fur Commission USA (Mink Farmers Research Foundation).

Mel H. Blanke
114 E. Mill Street
Plymouth, WI 53073
Notes: Legal Counsel for Fur Commission USA.

Kettle Moraine Mink Breeders Association (FFO)
N5350 Country Aire Road
Plymouth, WI 53073

Tony Pavek (FF-M) (FF-F)
W6220 Hwy. 64
Polar, WI 54418
Phone: (715) 627-7721
Contact: Tony Pavek, Todd Pavek
Notes: Located on north side of road, just west of 5th Avenue Road (east of the town of Polar).

Pavek (FF-M) (FF-F)
W6180 State Hwy 64
Polar, WI 54418

Brecke Mink Ranch; Stetsonville, Wisconsin

Patrick Fur Farm; Rib Lake, Wisconsin

Magnuson Fur Farm; Ogema, Wisconsin

Smieja Fur Farm; Independence, Wisconsin

Notes: The Pavek family owns several farms within several miles of this location.

Ethel B. Pavek (FF-M)
N3857 5th Avenue Road (alt. W6081 Hwy. 64)
Polar, WI 54418
Notes: Located at southeast corner of 5th Avenue Road and Hwy. 64. Farm may be closed (investigation needed).

Omega Mink Ranch (FF-M)
N3510 5th Avenue Road
Polar, WI 54418
Phone: (715) 627-4842 or (715) 623-3586
Contact: Guy & Mary Pavek
Notes: Sheds located on west side of road, at a distance from the road.

Kevin & Lisa Pavek (FF-M)
W6124 Hattes Lane
Polar, WI 54418
Phone: (715) 627-1280
Notes: Located off of 5th Avenue Road, approx. 1 mile south of Hwy. 64.

fur farm (FF-M)
3424 5th Ave
Polar, WI
Notes: Sheds at great distance from house. W side of road, before Hattes St.

fur farm (FF-M)
3222 5th Ave
Polar, WI
Notes: Status inconclusive. Two sheds set back from road. W side of road, after Hattes St. No house nearby.

Deerbrook Mink Ranch / Pavek Mink and Fox Farm (FF-M) (FF-F)
6081 Hwy 64
Polar, WI 54418
Robert T. Pavek.
Notes: Row of sheds S of house, slightly downhill. Visible from the beginning of 5th Ave, E side. Paperwork obtained lists this address as open, and as housing mink and fox. First name is from Secretary of State records, second from fur industry documents.

Gary Anzia (FF-M)
960 Lake Drive
Port Washington, WI 53704
Phone: (920) 689-4018 or (920) 284-6018
Contact: Gary & Sharon Anzia

Zwickey Fur Farm (FF-M)
6775 Ole Lake Road
Rhinelander, WI 54501
Phone: (715) 369-8986 or (715) 369-2308
Contact: Terry Berndt, Douglas Zwickey

Patrick Fur Farm (FF-M)
W3746 W Rib Road
Rib Lake, WI 54470
Phone: (715) 427-5260
Contact: Michael Patrick, Kyle Patrick
Notes: Located off of State Hwy. 102, south of the town center.

Zimbal Minkery (FF-M)
2111 Washington Avenue
Sheboygan, WI 53081
Phone: (920) 452-7380 or (920) 467-8125
Contact: Robert H. Zimbal
Notes: Located south of Washington Avenue at a distance, across railroad tracks. Very close to busy road and shopping

centers. Second location of the Zimbal Minkery. As many as 240,000 mink imprisoned between the two locations.

TMR Furs (FF-M)
N3481 County Road A
Sheboygan Falls, WI 53085
Phone: (920) 918-6764 or (920) 564-3115
Contact: Nick Trimberger, Gerard Trimberger
Notes: Located at corner of County Road A and Kurscheid Court.

Brecke Mink Ranch (FF-M)
N246 Oriole Drive
Stetsonville, WI 54480
Phone: (715) 678-2282
Contact: Edward & Ann Brecke
Notes: One of the largest fur farms in the country with 100,000 mink. E side of road. A few sheds directly on Oriole Drive. Rest set farm back from road. Sheds on Oriole are S of mailbox number 206. Many sheds set at quite a distance from the house.

North American Fur Auctions (FP)
205 Industrial Park Drive
Stoughton, WI 53589
Phone: (608) 205-9200
Fax: (608) 205-9210
Denis Schmitt: VP Ranch (fur farm) Relations
Greg Schroeder: US Trapper Relations Manager
Mike Balaam: Manager
Craig Oler: Maintenance / Supervisor
Laura Chicaizza: Assistant Manager
Brett Johnson: Maintenance Manager
Virgil Schroeder: Wild Fur Coordinator
Jim Posch: Mink Technical Manager

Dave Mengar: Shipping
Carmen Torres: Receiving
Amanda Bujosa: Ticketing
Mark Kubitz: Mink
Joe Poquette: Mink
Tom Gibson: Mink
Brian MacMillan: Wild Fur.
Michael Mengar: President and CEO
Notes: Perhaps the most significant choke point in the US fur industry, with hundreds of thousands of animal skins processed in this facility annually. The fur ranching and trapping industry relies on this facility to process raw skins, which are funneled through this building, processed, and then shippped to the NAFA auction house in Canada. Merged with American Legend / Seattle Fur Exchange in 2018, making the Canada location the only significant auction house in North American for farmed mink and fox. Stoughton is the head office and fur grading facility. NAFA is the largest seller of ranch raised mink and fox in North America. This location expanded its office and fur service processing facility in 2002. Buildings on either side Industrial Park Drive.

Walsh Mink Ranch (FF-M)
PO Box 101
Stratford, WI
Contact: Michael Walsh
Notes: Address unknown.

Nelson Mink Farm Inc (FF-M)
1500 Tacoma Beach Road 6 2
Sturgeon Bay, WI 54235
Notes: Incorporated in 2010. Address appears to be a residence. Uninvestigated.

Emulon Company
12408 Kr County Line Rd
Sturtevant, WI 53177
Notes: Possibly the nation's largest processor of mink oil. Several addresses in and around Kenosha. Address above is only one that appears capable of manufacturing, shipping, and/or receiving.

Arthur E. Modeen (FF-M)
4163 Hammond Ave.
Superior, WI 54880
Phone: (715) 394-3283

Sinac Mink Farm (FF-M)
N1435 Meridian Dr
Thorp, WI 54771
Notes: Recently constructed.

Ott's Mink Ranch (FF-M)
N10685 Red Pine Road
Tomahawk, WI 54487
Phone: (715) 453-8845
Contact: Alex & Jennifer Ott
Notes: Located off/east of Tannery Road, along railroad tracks.

Gessler's Pine Ridge Mink Ranch (FF-M)
N11856 Heafford Road
Tomahawk, WI 54487
Phone: (715) 453-5591
Contact: David Gessler
Notes: Located north of Beach Road. House on Heafford, sheds directly on Beach Rd (road for public beach access). Half block from a public park on one side, beachfront park on the other.

United Vaccines, Inc. (FR)
1131 Thousand Oaks Trail
Verona, WI 53593. (608) 276-5501.
Phone: (800) 283-6465 or (608) 276-5501
Contact: Wim Verhagen, CEO; Rebecca Kerns, Managing Director
Notes: New location as of 2018. Extremely significant to the mink industry as the last supplier of mink vaccines (Merck reportedly stopped supplying fur farmers several years ago). Each year a collective of mink farmers spend over $7 million in a bulk purchase from United Vaccines, which is the distributed to mink farmers. United Vaccines supplies vaccines to fur farmers in North America and Europe. Operates a production and research facility at the above address. The company has made statements to the media indicating research at the Verona address is conducted on "mice and other rodents." USDA documents indicate additional research at a mink facility in nearby, address unknown.

Thomas F. Hawe (FF-M)
N2594 Blueberry Lane
Waldo, WI 53093
Phone: (920) 528-8388
Notes: Tom Hawe died in July 2012. Farm may be closed (investigation needed).

Twardowski Farm (FF-F)
RR1 Box 707
Wabeno WI 54566
Contact: John Twardowski
Notes: Street address unknown.

fur farm (FF-M)
6376 Wisconsin 52
Wabeno, WI 54566
Notes: Several mink sheds visible from
road. Very small farm. Status unknown.

TMR Fur (FFFS)
Feed Building
W4941 County Road N
Waldo, WI 49805
Notes: Applied for permit to construct a
"feed building" at this address. This loca-
tion is 9 miles west of the TMR fur farm.
Also at this address: Rooker Pet Foods.

Thomas F. Hawe (FF-M)
N2594 Blueberry Lane
Waldo, WI 53093
Phone: (920) 528-8388
Notes: Tom Hawe died in July 2012.
Farm may be closed (investigation
needed).

Hillside Fox Ranch (FF-M) (FF-F)
W6779 Milligan Road
Waupun, WI 53963
Phone: (920) 324-3176
Contact: Lyle & Helen Bronkhorst
Notes: Located west of U.S. Highway
151, at corner of Milligan Road and
Business Highway 151/County Road M.
Pens set back from road, barely visible.
Very close to railroad tracks, which run
along the E.

Batten Farm (FF-F)
E2870 Goldsmith Road
Waupaca WI 54981
Contact: Kenneth Batten
Notes: Unconfirmed.

Roger Schroeder (FF-M)
5200 N 89th Street
Wausau, WI 54403
Phone: (715) 842-3681
Notes: Farm may be closed (investiga-
tion needed).

Samuel Schrock (FF-M)
W10181 Cumberland Road
Wautoma, WI 54982
Contact: Samuel & Carolyn Schrock
Notes: Small farm. Located just west of
County Road II.

Stan Jagler's Farm (FF-M)
West Bend, WI
Notes: Address unknown. Reported that
three young males "triggered alarm" in a
shed, 1998.

Patrick Fur Farm (FF-M)
W3746 W Rib Road
Westboro, WI 54490
Phone: (715) 427-5260
Contact: Michael Patrick
Notes: Large farm. Located off of State
Hwy. 102, south of the town center.
N side of road. Sheds directly on road.
Large property with several buildings
and trucks. "Patrick Fur Farm Inc" on
semi truck door. Sign on building reads
"Patrick Fur Farm, Fine Darks".

Zuleger Fur Farm (FF-F)
N7975 Zimmerman Road
Westboro, WI 54490
Phone: (715) 427-1002
Contact: Eric & Rebecca Zuleger
Notes: Located at southwest corner of
Zimmerman Road (NF-101) and Rindt
Road (NF-564). Rebecca Zuleger is Sec-
retary of the US Fox Shippers Council.

Golden Sands Ranch (FF-M)
N5183 17th Drive
Wild Rose, WI 54984
Phone: (920) 622-3338
Contact: Harry H. Erickson, Robert
Erickson
Notes: Large farm. Located between
County Road A and County Road O.

Kohl's Mink Ranch (FF-M)
Richard and Irene Kohl
Woodruff, WI
Notes: Address unknown.

Addendum

Closed Farm List
Small Farm List
Data Sources
Fur Farm Numbers
Most Wanted List

Closed Farm List

These farms were reported closed in the last decade. Farms are only reported closed when there is evidence beyond a reasonable doubt they are no longer in operation. Over 90 farms reported closed since 2010.

Arkansas

Elmore Farm
1400 Hwy 96 W
Mansfield, AR 72944

Illinois

Zuchel Farm
18207 Collins Road
Woodstock, IL 60098

Sorensen Mink Farm
19014 Kishwaukee Valley Rd.
Marengo, IL 60152

Charles Ide Jr.
8250 Edgewood Drive (off of 83rd Street)
Downers Grove, IL 60516
Notes: Farm reported closed. One of the oldest farms in the country, founded in 1932.

Indiana

Adams Fox & Mink Ranch
2814 East 150 South
Anderson, IN 46017

Owl Creek Fox Farm
8343 S 1000 W
Montpelier, IN 47359

Iowa

Diamond V Mills
838 1st Street NW
Cedar Rapids, IA 52407

Notes: According to sattelite images,this building was demolished. Relocated?

Palmer Erickson
3374 Saratoga Avenue
Jewell, IA 50130
Notes: Palmer Erickson died in 2012 and this farm appears to be closed.

Roger Harms
3201 200th Avenue
Titonka, IA 50480

Conger Farm
26381 295th Street
Ollie, IA 52576

Paul Shunkwiler
2605 Hwy. 9
Osage, IA 50461

Maryland

Parsons Mink Ranch
7765 Jersey Rd. Box 304.
Salisbury, MD 21801

Massachusetts

Berkshire Furs
172 Peru Road / County Road 143
Hinsdale, MA 01235
Farm reported closed in January 2010.

Carmel Mink Ranch
172 Peru Road / County Road 143

Hinsdale, MA 01235
Notes: Reportedly "pelted out," summer 2010.

Michigan

fur farm
2495 Phaneuf
Traverse City, MI 49686

Jack Brower Fur Farm
15011 Chandler Road
Bath, MI 48808

Minnesota

North Branch Fur Farm
County Road 15
North Branch, MN 55056
Phone: (651) 674-4721

Gunnink Fur Farm
446 80th Avenue
Chandler, MN 56122
Phone: (507) 677-2223
Notes: Farm reported closed in on-site investigation.

Anderson Mink Farm
4515 292nd Street E.
Randolph, MN 55065

Davidson Fur Farm
10739 30th Street NW
Annandale, MN 55302

Petersen Fur Farm
10587 Tagus Avenue
Brownton, MN 55312

Randall Knudsen
52655 780th Avenue
Buffalo Lake, MN 55324

Warner's Westside Fur Farm
59483 Csah 11
Litchfield, MN 55355

Paul Hegge
19041 Hegge Drive
Spring Grove, MN 55974

Gimble Mink Ranch
19104 Mink Drive
Spring Grove, MN 55974

Hillcrest Mink Ranch
28774 State Highway 34
Detroit Lakes, MN 56501

Fur farm
37110 800th Street/County
Road 12
Okabena, MN

Fur farm
7009 110th Avenue NW
Byron, MN

Montana

George Lentz
1920 Whitefish Stage Road
Kalispell, MT 59901

Cole L Mcpherson
16350 US Highway 12 W
(Lolo
Creek Road)
Lolo, MT 59847
Notes: Reported as empty,
summer 2012. McPherson
maintains a captive wildlife
permit, possibly for other
species.

Behling Fox Farm
3523 McIntosh Lane
Darby, MT 59829
Nebraska

Merck Animal Health
Elkhorn Biotechnology
Excellence Center
21401 W. Center Road
Elkhorn, NE 68022
Notes: Reports state that
Merck stopped producing
the vaccine, leaving only
United Vaccines as a source
for mink vaccines.

New York

McKean Farm
291 State Route 79
Windsor, NY 13865

Marr's Fur & Game Farm
4964 E Swamp Road
Stanley, NY 14561

Reader Fur Farm
7850 Route 5 and 20
East Bloomfield, NY 14469

Main Mink Ranch
Route 60
Gerry, NY 14740

Peters Fur Farm
5681 Southwestern Blvd.
Hamburg, NY 14075

Nettleton Mink Farm
12 Slate Hill Road
Spencertown, NY 12165

Bennett Farms
2321 State Route 64
Bloomfield, NY 14469
Notes: Confirmed closed,
January 2010.

North Carolina

Carolina Fur Farm, Inc.
417 Garden Valley Road
Statesville NC 28625

North Dakota

Schultz Fur Farm
13392 29th Street NW
Arnegard, ND 58835
Notes: Bobcat farm, relocated to Montana.

Ohio

Silver Gates Fur Farm
17822 Township Road 104
Kenton, OH 43326

Browns Fox Ranch
9477 Hicksville Edgerton
Hicksville, OH 43526

Haska Fur Farm
6991 Hughes Road
Ravenna, OH 44266

Darrell Robbins
Rural Route 1
(alternate address: 3262
Road 204)
Antwerp, OH 45813

Mohoric Mink Ranch
7035 Chatham Road
Medina, OH 44256

Oregon

Diehl-Filliger
84703 Junction Rd.
Seaside, OR 97138
Status: Reported closed via
anonymous report, summer
2010.

Closed farm, Oregon

Closed Roger Kubitz farm; Athens, Wisconsin

Closed farm, Utah

Fox @ now-closed Palmer Erickson farm; Jewel, Iowa

Ylipelto's Fur Farm
92659 Simonsen Loop Road
Astoria, OR 97103
Notes: Reported closed via
media reports, July 2010.

Pennsylvania

Burns Mink Ranch
119 Bend Road
New Wilmington, PA 16142
Phone: (724) 946-3125
Contact: John Burns

South Dakota

Don Dargatz
13367 446th Avenue
Waubay, SD 57273

Classic Farm
38495 283rd Street
Armour, SD 57313
Contact: Les Groeneweg,
Manager

Utah

Black Willow Mink
340 N. Main Street
Coalville, UT 84017

fur farm
1160 N Main St
Lewiston, UT
Notes: Confirmed closed,
2010

D J Mink
800 N Morgan Valley Drive
Morgan, UT 84050

Ken A. Durrant
210 S. Morgan Valley Drive
Morgan, UT 84050

Lyle Allen Groves
11454 S 1300 W
South Jordan, UT 84095
Notes: Farm confirmed
closed (April 2010).

fur farm
2085 S Morgan Valley Drive
Morgan, UT 84050

Seth Dawson
84 W 200 N
Morgan, UT 84050

Fort Creek Mink Ranch
3078 W. State Road 32
Peoa, UT 84061

D&B Fur Farm
5434 N. Woodenshoe Lane
Peoa, UT 84061

Lake Shore Mink Ranch
90 W Church Road
Toole, UT 84074

Mark Klotovich
1546 W 8600 S
West Jordan, UT 84084

Holt Mink Ranch
10291 S 1230 W
South Jordan, UT 84095

Lynn Allen Groves
11454 S 1300 W
South Jordan UT 84095

Bytheway Mink Ranch
2011 S 1600 W
Lewiston, UT 84320

Kevin Petersen Ranch
1560 S Main Street
Lewiston, UT 84320

North Forty Mink Ranch
11611 N Hwy. 91
Richmond, UT 84333

Rees' Mink Ranch
600 Icy Springs Road
Coalville, UT 84017

Kenneth Vernon Mink
Ranch
285 E. Center Street
Woodruff, UT 84086

Pace Ranch (FF-M)
4950 S. Hollow Road
Logan, UT 84321
Notes: No farm visible from
road.

Utah State University
North Logan Farms
1475 N 800 E
Logan, UT 84341
Notes: This one-time "hub"
of Aleutian disease research
may no longer experiment
on mink. 2011 USDA re-
cords do not reflect mink are
used at USU. Fur industry
researcher LeGrande Ellis
died in 2008.

Willow Valley
7145 N 6720 W
American Fork, UT 84003

Virginia

D & S Fox Farm
16671 Fox Farm Lane
Elkton, VA 22827

Washington

Erwin G. Joedicke
919 288th St NW
Arlington, WA 98223-9181

Luna Rose Farm
6422 SW 110th Avenue
Olympia, WA 98512

Brainard Mink Ranch
19127 Welch Road
Snohomish, WA 98290
Notes: Reported closed
(summer 2011).

American Legend Cooperative / Seattle Fur Exchange
200 SW 34th Street
Renton, WA 98055
Notes: At one time, American Legend had more
than 200 member-owners,
approximately one-third
in Canada and the rest in
the United States, and was
"North America's largest fur
auction house, selling over
70% of the North American mink crop annually."
Merged with NAFA, 2018.

Blue Granite Fur Farm
7715 Robe Menzel Road
Granite Falls, WA 98252

Olsen Mink Ranch
4695 Reese Hill Road
Sumas, WA 98295

Wisconsin

Burg Bros. Mink Ranch
W5450 Ecker Lakeland
Chilton, WI 53014

Bartel & Winkel
W976 County Road HHH
Chilton, WI 53014

Wyndway Mink Ranch
N5512 County Road S
Lake Mills, WI 53551

Mark Hansen
N7243 N. Crystal Lake
Beaver Dam, WI 53916

Pavek Mink & Fox Ranch
N5211 Rosedale Road
Deerbrook, WI 54424

Henry & Patricia Deml, Inc.
N2375 Hemlock Drive
Medford, WI 54451

Patrick Fur Farm
N7097 County Road C
Rib Lake, WI 54470

Ken Holmes Mink Ranch
W8956 County Road M
Medford, WI 54451
Notes: Sattelite images indicate this farm is closed.

Romie Deml Mink Ranch
N3641County Road E
Medford, WI 54451

Albers Mink Ranch
W5299 Pleasant Avenue
Medford, WI 54451

Ames Mink Farm
9879 Siemering Drive
Tomahawk, WI 54487

Zwickey Fur Farm
6775 Ole Lake Road
Rhinelander, WI 54501

Chartier Fur Farm
13901 Moss Lake Drive
Lac Du Flambeau, WI
54538

Somo Fur Ranch
W12081 Barneys Drive
Tripoli, WI 54564

Northwest Mink Ranch
N4533 Zebro Road
Bruce, WI 54819
Phone: (715) 868-3581
Hans Haugen
Status: Confirmed

Brown's Mink Ranch
3457 Riverside Drive
Beloit WI 53511

O.J. Krull & Sons Fur Farm
W5188 Rock Road
Black Creek, WI 54106
(alternate address: 4140 N.
Richmond Street, Appleton,
WI 54913)

Kornuth Mink Ranch
W9401 Hobbles Creek
Road
Catawba, WI 54515

Fox farm
7805 Cheese Factory Road
Iron River, WI 54847

Fur Farm
Grandview Road
Verona, WI 53593

Steinhardt Farms Inc
845 South Street
Plymouth WI 53073-2459

Small Farm List
The smallest farms known to exist

In the 1990s, mink farms with 2 or 3,000 animals were not uncommon (fox farms generally imprison animals in the dozens or low-hundreds).

Since then, the consolidation in the fur industry has been tremendous. Smaller farms have closed, and the large have gotten larger.

Today, it is rare to find mink farms with fewer than 5,000 animals. Farmers who operate at this level generally do so more as a hobby or side business than as a primary source of income.

A list of the smallest mink farms known in the US:

> North Star Fur Farm (Ollie, IA)
> Misty Moonlight Mink Ranch (Waverly, IA)
> J & G Mink Ranch (Highland, UT)
> Ovard Mink Farm (Wanship, UT)
> McMullin Fur Farm (South Jordan, UT)
> Scott & Amber McGee (Skandia, MI)
> Pelton Fur Farm (Rome, NY)
> Jefferson Fur Farm (Jefferson, OR)
> Willes Fur Farm (Lehi, UT)
> Van Dyke Mink Farm (Springville UT)
> Sherfield Farm (Butternut WI)
> Sally Costabile (Kenosha, WI)
> Samuel Schrock (Wautoma, WI)

In addition, numerous micro-farms can be seen around Franklin Utah; however most are unconfirmed.

Small farms generally are the first to go out of business when the industry weakens, and with recent industry turmoil it is likely some of these farms have closed.

Data Sources

Credit for all data in *The Blueprint* goes to these sources:

Operation Bite Back: It is believed that addresses and other documents obtained from raids of fur research labs during Operation Bite Back were a primary source in the creation of the first widely circulated fur farm list, The Final Nail #1.

Coalition To Abolish Fur Farms: CAFF circulated early fur farm lists and previously unknown data in the early-1990s. The information was also incorporated into The Final Nail #1 and subsequent fur farm lists (like this one).

Coalition To Abolish The Fur Trade (CAFT): In the 1990s, CAFT publicized much of the analysis of industry weaknesses that you read in these page. Without CAFT's difficult work of poring over industry documents, infiltrating industry events, and more; we would know far less about the weak links in US fur farming.

The Final Nail **(publication):** The original fur farm list. The Final Nail formed the basis for all fur farm intelligence to come. It's speculated The Final Nail is the product of documents taken from fur industry targets during the ALF's "Operation Bite Back" campaign in the early 1990s. To date, The Final Nail is on its 4th edition. Each new edition brings to light new fur industry information that often could only be known by those who have worked under darkness and obtained the information illicitly. As such, The Final Nail has always been published anonymously.

FinalNail.com (website): The majority of new information here can be credited to the researchers at FinalNail.com, an online directory of fur farms, lab animal suppliers, and slaughterhouses. Since the mid-2000s, FinalNail.com has been the largest contributor to new fur farm discovery. Most of the new information contained in this updated Blueprint was first made public on FinalNail.com.

The Fur Farm Intelligence Project: Along with others, I organized the FFIP in 2009 to visit the majority of fur farms in the US, determine their operational status, and combine with other source to create the first major fur farm list update in over a decade. The project took us to over 200 farms across the country, gathering information on new addresses and the current status of known farms and other industry targets.

Coalition Against Fur Farms: After the conclusion of the time-specific Fur Farm Intelligence Project, some volunteers opted to turn the FFIP into an ongoing one, and launched CAFF (a slight variation of "Coalition To Abolish Fur Farms," a 90s group with the same mission). Today, CAFF exists primarily as a website, tracking new discoveries in fur industry intelligence, including address changes, farm closures, leaked industry documents, and more.

Anonymous activists: Much, if not most new information collected over the past 10 years was submitted anonymously to both FinalNail.com, CAFF and other groups, and subsequently made public. These anonymous submissions take many forms. One, digital documents and emails submitted anonymously. Two, anonymous data collection efforts, the fruits of which can only be speculated to percolate up to aboveground activists either directly or indirectly. Some examples include the aforementioned Operation Bite Back campaign, and the break-in at the Hawkeye Mink Cooperative (in which several duffel bags of documents were stolen in an overnight action).

As stated, the largest contributions to this document come from the aforementioned sources, and their research methods may vary.

In my personal work to compile both the original and updated *Blueprint*, I relied on the following:

On-site investigations
Over 200 farms - opened and closed - were visited during the two month road phase of the original Fur Farm Intelligence Project that was the impetus for *The Blueprint*.

Satellite images
Used primarily to verify the presence (or appearance) of animal sheds or pens at addresses obtained post-road-trip phase.

Business entity records
Secretary of State's office records which give clues to a business's operational status were referenced.

Media reports
Old and recent media reports on the fur industry provided many addresses.

Business directories

Fur industry trade journals

and...

Anonymous Submissions

As word on our work compiling original *The Blueprint* spread, we were provided with a box of documents from inside the fur industry. This paperwork was never intended for public circulation. These documents, ranging in date from 1998 to July, 2009 - were a trove of new addresses and other unpublished info. Among the documents were a fur farm mailing list, memos, business cards, and other paperwork providing leads on unknown farms.

In addition, several anonymous reports were submitted detailing specific sites. When still relevant, those reports are being included in this updated *Blueprint*.

Hawkeye Mink Coop, Jewel Iowa
Thousands of documents confiscated in overnight break-in (2002)

Fur Farm Numbers
Tracking The Truth

How many fur farms are there? Short answer: No one knows.

For mink farms, the last year the USDA tracked the number of farms was 2011, when it reported 268 mink farms in the United States.

For many reasons, this figure is likely to be wildly inaccurate, as the fur farm industry is largely untracked.

For one, many farms fly under the radar. The USDA relies on state (as well as other) data, and the degree to which states tracks farms in their state vary widely.

Two, there is even less reliable numbers for fox and other "fur bearing" species. These farms are entirely untracked on the federal level, and their tracking on the state level varies from "barely" to "not at all."

I personally filed public records requests to 40 states requesting addresses for all farms which house or breed mink, foxes, bobcats, and/or lynx. I then compared the results against the fur farm list in *The Blueprint*. Of the 200+ known farms I found that states revealed less than 10 of them.

Drawing from sources in recent history, we have some rough numbers to use as a basis for forming an estimate.

At one time the Fur Commission USA advertised they represented "over 400 farming families working on close to 300 farms in about two dozen states." This is likely to be somewhere in range of the total number of professional-level (vs. hobby level) fur farms.

But that was 2013. Today, any mention of farm numbers has been removed from their literature, possibly indicating a severe drop they don't wish to publicize.

The number of mink farms reported by the USDA dropped over 75% from the late 1980s until the last reported statistics in 2011. With prices at an all time low and the industry in a crisis as this goes to press, that drop in farms is expected to be even more severe today.

Again, fox farming (and farms imprisoning other species) have no national trade group dedicated to them, and there is very little known about farm numbers in these niche industries.

For a more detailed analysis of how little farm numbers are tracked, the following article from wildlife advocacy group Born Free USA provides a brief analysis of how little we know about the true number of fur farms.

U.S. Fur Farm Numbers
by Born Free USA

The USDA National Agricultural Statistics Service (NASS) collects data on the number of mink farms, the number of mink pelts produced broken down by color class, value of pelts, and the number of female mink bred, and the percentage of each fur color class the females were bred to produce. This information is compiled in an annual market report as are other agricultural commodities. The NASS does not collect data on farmed fox, lynx, or bobcat fur production.

According to the NASS, mink production reports are based on "a census of all known active producers."

The list of "active producers" is compiled from "various sources" and the census is conducted via mail or telephone. In most cases NASS representatives do not actually visit the farms in the course of the census (pers. comm. Chris Hawthorn USDA 06/25/09).

According to the 2008 census there were between 274 and 283 mink farms in the United States. However these numbers may not tell the whole story.

Most states where fur farms exist don't require farms to be licensed and state agriculture departments may not even be aware of the location, status, or existence of some farms. It is also possible that the NASS has knowledge of fur farms that the state agriculture or wildlife agencies are unaware of (pers. comm. Hawthorn).

Independent surveys (counting mink, fox, and lynx/bobcat farms) indicate there are significantly more fur farms in many states than are reported in the NASS. While the presence of fox and lynx/bobcat farms in alternative data explains some of the discrepancy, the alternative data also indicate a greater number of mink farms.

Some differences in numbers may be the result of how farms are counted. The NASS data do not distinguish between single location farms and farms with multiple locations; the data collected are entirely dependent upon how the producer collects data. So if a producer operates three farms but records the data collectively, the three farms are counted as one, but if the producer keeps separate records for each farm and reports each of them, the farms would be counted individually (pers. comm. Hawthorn).

Some variation in data may also be explained by lack of disclosure. The NASS records nine farms as being assigned to "other states" when in fact the information is not from farms in "other states" at all, but from states listed in the report that were counted differently to "avoid disclosing individual operations."

Additional discrepancies can be found in the estimates of total number of mink pelts produced. The NASS reported that in 2007 a total of 2.83 million mink pelts were produced (USDA 2009). Data from the Fur Commission USA sourced from Oslo Fur Auctions estimate 3 million farmed mink pelts were produced that year (Fur Commission 2007). This amounts to hundreds of thousands of mink pelts possibly uncounted for by the USDA, further calling into question the accuracy of the USDA's annual mink report.

The NASS has also begun reducing the amount of data collected and published. The NASS used to note the total number of U.S. mink farms that also reported raising fox (although these data were never broken down by state or fur value). In 2006, 16 mink farms reported also raising fox (down from 19 in 2005). However, the 2007 NASS report contained a "special note" informing that "the number of mink farms also raising fox will no longer be published." Another "special note" included in the 2008 NASS report (released July 10, 2009) stated, "The number of operations by state will no longer be published on an annual basis. State level numbers will only be published in conjunction with the Census of Agriculture every five years. The number of operations at the U.S. level will continue to be published on an annual basis" (USDA 2009).

Update: The USDA stopped reporting mink farm numbers in 2011.

Most Wanted List
Top 3 Undiscovered Targets

The list represents the most sensitive fur industry targets which remain undiscovered.

#1: United Vaccines mink research
One USDA document references an inspection at a "naïve mink" facility in Blue Mounds, WI (near its Verona facility). Its exact location remains undiscovered. The significance of United Vaccines in the global fur trade makes this facility an important target.

#2: Idaho State University mink research
The location of Jack Rose's mink research remains a mystery. One of the few facilities in the US confirmed to still imprison mink.

#3: National Feeds mink research
This large feed supplier formerly operated an experimental mink farm in Oshkosh, WI. It is possible National Feeds has ceased research altogether. Because this company is a large feed supplier, it is also possible the farm relocated and awaits discovery.

Additionally, the following subjects are of particular interest because info is scarce:

- Lynx & bobcat farm addresses
- Fox farm addresses
- Unknown research sites

All information on unknown fur farms and fur industry targets should be submitted to whistleblower@coalitionagainstfurfarms.com

Adopt A Fur Farm
Investigators Wanted

To keep future editions of *The Blueprint* as accurate as possible, we need your help.

Drive to every fur farm within driving distance, and document the following:

- Is the farm open or closed?
- Does it imprison species not currently listed?
- Any other relevant details.

Then submit any and all information gathered to:

whistleblower@coalitionagainstfurfarms.com

Further Research

www.FinalNail.com

www.CoalitionAgainstFurFarms.com

LIBERATE

STORIES & LESSONS ON ANIMAL
LIBERATION ABOVE THE LAW

PETER YOUNG

At various times, Peter Young has been a fugitive, protester, author, prisoner, felon, spokesperson, entrepreneur, hobo, saboteur, publisher, speaker, and criminal of conscience.

By various federal agencies and trade groups, he has been called a terrorist, eco-terrorist, domestic terrorist, "special interest" terrorist, burglar, accessory after the fact, danger to the community, armed and dangerous, flight risk, escape risk, and unindicted co-conspirator.

Today he runs internet businesses and continues his lifelong, unbroken succession of conspiracies.

He can be contacted at:
peter@peteryoung.me

www.ingramcontent.com/pod-product-compliance
Lightning Source LLC
Chambersburg PA
CBHW032112280326

41933CB00009B/804